"Our culture brainwashes us to think that greed is the motivation that drives us, but this book offers a powerful alternative message—the transformative power of generosity. This message could literally change the world, beginning with your life and mine."

— BRIAN D. MCLAREN
author of *The Great
Spiritual Migration*

"More and more churches understand that in order to effectively preach the gospel, we must also live the gospel. In contrast to the societal value of gaining and collecting power, privilege, and wealth, this book documents the story of a church that opted to give away their possessions. Their example reminds us that the New Testament church is alive and well and that there could be the possibility of a movement of generous churches."

— SOONG-CHAN RAH
author of *The Next Evangelicalism*
and *Prophetic Lament*

"Along with the modern stories of LaSalle, the authors effectively interlace ancient stories from the Bible and advice from outside resources, financial and religious. They write as much about the grinding, rewarding process of discernment—praying, meeting, listening inside and out—as about dispersal of funds. Part story of LaSalle's decision of how to handle their investment, part testament to the powers of generosity, this book will be of interest to anyone interested in community building or philanthropy."

— *Publishers Weekly*

LOVE

Radical Generosity for the Real World

LET

Laura Sumner Truax & Amalya Campbell

GO

WILLIAM B. EERDMANS PUBLISHING COMPANY
Grand Rapids, Michigan

WM. B. EERDMANS PUBLISHING CO.
2140 Oak Industrial Drive N.E., Grand Rapids, Michigan 49505
www.eerdmans.com

23 22 21 20 19 18 17   1 2 3 4 5 6 7

ISBN 978-0-8028-7447-4

Library of Congress Cataloging-in-Publication Data

Names: Truax, Laura Sumner, 1961– author.
Title: Love let go : radical generosity for the real world / Laura Sumner Truax &
  Amalya Campbell.
Description: Grand Rapids : Eerdmans Publishing Co., 2017. | Includes
  bibliographical references.
Identifiers: LCCN 2016046689 | ISBN 9780802874474 (hardcover : alk. paper)
Subjects: LCSH: Generosity—Religious aspects—Christianity.
Classification: LCC BV4647.G45 T78 2017 | DDC 241/.4—dc23
  LC record vailable at https://lccn.loc.gov/2016046689

To the people of LaSalle Street Church,
past, present, and future

Contents

Foreword, *by Richard Stearns*   ix

I

OUR GENEROUS NATURE

1. Wired to Be Givers   3
2. The Plane of Generosity   21
3. Abundance, Not Scarcity   39

II

STUMBLING TOWARD GENEROSITY

4. Identity Intact   61
5. Transactions and Interactions   77
6. The Saturation Point   95

III

THE GENEROUS LIFE

7. Listening Inside Out   115
8. Listening Outside In   135
9. Reframing Thankfulness   153
10. Letting Love Go   167

CONTENTS

Afterword   183

Questions for Reflection and Discussion   185

For Further Reading   196

Notes   198

Acknowledgments   202

FOREWORD

While visiting a Syrian refugee settlement in Lebanon with Laura Truax in May 2016, I gained an appreciation for Laura's passion for generosity. This is the generosity she explores in this book with co-author Ami Campbell; the two share their insight into the kind of radical generosity that brings unexpected freedom to our lives. My own experience with this started almost thirty years ago.

In October 1987, I was working in the corporate world when "Black Monday" struck—the largest single-day stock market crash in history. In one fell swoop, my wife, Reneé, and I lost a third of our life savings as well as the money we'd put away for our children's college education. I was horrified.

Since I had grown up in poverty, my hard-won financial health was very important to me—even more with a young family to support. I became a man obsessed with finances. The next few days were a blur of late-night agonizing over what we'd lost followed by morning calls to sell off our remaining holdings (which only made things worse).

Reneé saw that in my anguish I was allowing money to control me. One night she sat down beside me as I labored over my spreadsheets. She pointed out all the good things we had to be thankful for. "You need to let go of this and trust God," she said gently. She suggested we pray together. Amazingly, I hadn't thought to seek God in my distress.

After we prayed, Reneé shocked me by proposing that we pull out the checkbook and write some sizeable checks—amounting to about one-third of what we'd lost—to our church and the other ministries we support. She explained, "We need to show God that we know this is his money and not ours."

Once the checks were signed, sealed, and ready to send, I felt a wave of relief—the spell that money had cast over me was broken. It was a leap of faith that felt crazy at the time, but God blessed us. Specifically, I believe God was preparing me to make the difficult but rewarding choice ten years later to join World Vision and take a significant pay cut. I'd learned that I could trust God for the outcome.

My story would fit very well in this book. Laura and Ami explore the notion that practicing generosity—putting money in its proper place in our life of faith—frees us. It happened for LaSalle Street Church in Chicago; it happens for you and me.

God intends giving to be an act of faith and a sign of our dependence. In Old Testament times, people were obligated to pledge the first fruits of their harvest as an offering to God, in thanks and remembrance for God delivering them from slavery in Egypt. This meant giving from the *first* harvest, at a time when people couldn't be sure there would be a second. In other words, it was fruit of survival, not surplus.

Today there's no such law governing our income or "harvests," although diligent tithing continues to be integral to spiritual health, keeping us grounded in what's really important in our lives. As Jesus so aptly said, "For where your treasure is, there your heart will be also" (Matt. 6:21).

Generosity is also revitalizing for a church, and in my experience, that's true of congregations around the world. In addition to the example of LaSalle Street Church you're about to read, I've visited tiny churches in rural Africa that blossomed once they overcame the stigma of AIDS and started pouring themselves out for their neighbors through their time, talent, and treasure. I've seen churches in both hemispheres, rich and poor, flourish as they spread out beyond their four walls to share Jesus's love with the most vulnerable people, locally and globally.

After all, the poverty and disparity in our world today are not what God intended. In the economics of the kingdom, all would give equally, and there would be enough for everyone. But we've fallen short. I believe God is calling us to right the balance on behalf of the suffering people he loves.

The average giving of Christians in the U.S. is 2.4 percent of our income. If we increased our giving by just 1 percent—each of us giving just 60 cents a day more—that would generate enough money year after year to accomplish amazing things. That small change alone would have the power to wipe out extreme poverty in the world in just a generation. It's a stunning realization. In twenty years, we could could tackle clean water, hunger, preventable diseases, education, and capital for small businesses. And we'd still have billions left over.

As Laura and Ami share in this book, our journey of generosity is framed by God's big story of creating us, his children, and giving us everything we need to prosper. I believe an important part of this story is that God so loved us, he sent his only Son, who then commissions us to continue his work: "As the Father has sent me, I am sending you" (John 20:21). This is an invitation to become God's partners in restoring, reforming, and redeeming a broken world. In order to obey, we need to be willing to lay down all we are and all we have—all the resources he entrusted to us—for the kingdom.

I and many others who have said "yes" to that invitation can tell you that it's a thrilling adventure. Changing the world isn't easy, and it doesn't come cheap. But what an incredible privilege it is to be chosen and equipped for this purpose by our loving God.

RICHARD STEARNS
president of World Vision U.S.
and author of *The Hole in Our Gospel*

I

OUR GENEROUS NATURE

CHAPTER 1

WIRED TO BE GIVERS

All of us have a super-power capable of improving almost every aspect of our lives. This power is so potent that it virtually guarantees a better life. We *flourish* when we use this power. And not just us. All those around us flourish as well. It's strong enough to affect the behaviors of our friends . . . and even *the friends of our friends.*

When we use this power, studies show, we have increased energy, empathy, and happiness. Not only that, but this power is regenerative. The more we use it, the more we have. These results are as conclusive as the link between exercise and health, as indisputable as the relationship of sleep to mental alertness. It's amazing.

Equally amazing is that most of us simply don't believe it. Even with all the academic research, the steady stream of popular press, and the wisdom of the ages, for the vast majority of us this power is just lying there—impotent—all because we don't use it.

What is this super-power?

Generosity.

Generosity seems so old-school, so decidedly boring. It's easy to think that researchers have gotten it wrong—or at least have overstated the benefits of a humdrum virtue.

Sociologist Christian Smith describes generosity as "the virtue of giving good things to others freely and abundantly."[1] Sounds nice. But what's super-powerish about that?

Generosity may look simple on the surface, but it's fairly complex when we shift to deeper examination. Generosity is the belief that we have something of value to give to others *and* that we can give it freely and easily.

> Generosity may look simple on the surface, but it's fairly complex when we shift to deeper examination.

That's it. Sounds pretty straightforward. Yet the definition implies that we've done several key things:

- taken a personal inventory of our time, energy, relationships, financial resources, and professional talents
- clearly understood the resources we've cultivated
- assigned values to those resources
- decided that these resources have meaning and, through our sharing them, are important—not just for ourselves but for others
- become and remained self-aware and aware of others—to

the point that we are able to see what they lack, need, or appreciate

The relationship of giving to receiving is a paradoxical one because at least on the surface, doesn't it appear we *lose* something when we give it away? If I "spend" an hour with a friend discussing her life, doesn't that mean I have one less hour to "spend" on myself? Likewise, doesn't giving fifty dollars to a cause make our wallets lighter, not heavier? Are we just playing word games to say that "in giving we receive"? After all, who hasn't heard the common-sense wisdom of "Put your own oxygen mask on first!" and "You can't care for others if you haven't cared for yourself!" How can giving to others benefit us so directly?

The relationship of giving to receiving is a paradoxical one because at least on the surface, doesn't it appear we lose something when we give it away?

Given generosity's explosive potential, it's no surprise that it's one of the hottest research topics in social science right now. The University of Notre Dame (aka "The Fighting Irish") has an entire academic center on the science of generosity that is "fighting for a more generous world" by bringing a host of disciplines together to determine the causes, mechanisms, and consequences of generosity. It didn't take long for two researchers from the Center, Smith and Hilary Davidson, to

identify some desirable qualities to which generosity is posi-
tively linked:[2] Generous people are more likely to be happier
and healthier. They are not only less likely to be depressed;
they are also more likely to live with a deep sense of purpose.

When Smith and Davidson defined generosity, they exam-
ined all the ways we offer ourselves and our abilities to others.
But Harvard Business School professor Michael Norton and
University of British Columbia psychology professor Elizabeth
Dunn narrowed their focus to just financial generosity. Their
finding? Money can buy happiness . . . *just as long as we spend
the money on others.*[3] That may seem obvious if we're thinking
about the pleasure we get when we purchase and give someone
we love a gift that they love. But in their book *Happy Money*,
Norton and Dunn explain that they discovered something far
more interesting—something
that might just change the
annual office party forever.

> Money can buy happiness
> . . . just as long as we spend
> the money on others.

In a variety of experi-
ments, their research team
gave free money to sports clubs, sales teams, and randomly
chosen individuals. Some of the recipients were given the
freedom to spend the money on whatever they wanted. Others were given the freedom to spend the money however they
chose *as long as they spent it on others.* Each group had to spend
or give away the money within a specified window of time.

Repeatedly the salespeople *made more sales* when they

were told to give the money away rather than purchase something for themselves. The intramural sports teams *dominated their league*, winning 25 percent more games than those teams who kept the money. Consistently, individuals and groups said they were happier and felt closer to their friends and colleagues when they gave to others—even to people they didn't know.

Furthermore, Norton and Dunn found these conclusions hold true all over the world, in country after country. Spending on others makes us happier than spending on ourselves. Generosity is a simple, compelling truth. It's also a universal truth.

The Gallup World Poll, produced by the giant public polling agency, routinely surveys samples of people in 136 countries from around the world. Between 2006 and 2008, more than 200,000 respondents completed surveys on a range of issues relating to generosity and their satisfaction with life, and in 120 out of 136 countries, respondents who gave money away were happier. In fact, people felt as happy giving away money as they did about an increase in their household income. As Norton and Dunn note, the relationship "held up even after controlling for individuals' income. Across the 136 countries . . . *donating to charity had a similar relationship to happiness as doubling household income.*"[4]

Generosity is a simple, compelling truth. It's also a universal truth.

That's crazy! Yes. And transformational! The benefits of a generous life are demonstrative, verifiable, and authentic. And they're all right within our grasp—no matter how little or how much we have. At the end of the day, we seem to be hard-wired to give. But what happens when that hard-wiring is challenged? When doubts surface? When we hold back, rather than share? Just because we're hard-wired to give doesn't mean that generosity is easy.

The benefits of a generous life are demonstrative, verifiable, and authentic. And they're all right within our grasp—no matter how little or how much we have.

The Challenge to Give

On a clear day in September 2014, more than three hundred people made their way to a downtown Chicago church for what they expected to be a typical Sunday service. Hours later they emerged from the doors of the church surprised, perplexed, excited, and nervous. Each gripping a $500 check given with one short sentence of instruction: "Do good in the world."

That urban church held to the principle that all of us are wired to give—and that intentional generosity can change a church's relationship with its community, the city, and the world. But even while holding to that principle, the church faced challenges.

A few weeks earlier, church leaders had received an email detailing the sale of a long-ago real estate investment named Atrium Village. The church had joined with other faith communities in the 1970s to build some desperately needed low-income housing. Now, thirty-five years later, the property was being sold. The communication was concise and to the point:

> . . . Atrium Village has closed. The Board has just met and authorized . . . a check or wire to each of the four churches in the amount of $1,530,116.78. Hallelujah!

One of the four churches was ours—LaSalle Street Church. And while some of us in leadership had known the money was coming, now here it was. Literally. "Our" money was in our bank account. We spent the next few hours giddily sharing the news with the rest of the church board in emails with lots of exclamation points and smiley faces. But within the next few days we started to get serious. This was *a lot* of money. We decided as a church board to take a few weeks to process the news just among ourselves. Because it was the middle of summer, with many members and staff on vacation for weeks at a time, we chose to hold the big announcement to the church until the first week of September, when the fall programs would begin.

But waiting to make the big announcement didn't mean we were waiting to discuss how that money would be spent. This sum—which ultimately rose to $1.6 million, roughly double our annual budget—came during a time of acute financial pressure. Just a month earlier we had stood in front of our congregation and informed them of a fifty-thousand-dollar deficit. We had already cut our operating expenses as much as possible. We knew we might have to reduce staff hours. Additionally, we struggled with the loss of access to a neighborhood parking facility. The prudent side of us knew that this new windfall shouldn't be used to plug a hole in the budget or mask unsustainable aspirations. We understood that. But still, looking at all that money did make us wonder if perhaps *just a little* could be set aside for our operating expenses . . . just this once?

Within weeks, simmering discontents and disagreements over past decisions started to fester among our leadership team. *Why was our church staff so large in the first place? Just what do they do all day? Why hadn't we secured parking earlier?* Some of us (the more fiscally liberal) got defensive. The penny-pinchers got a wee bit righteous. Many of us found ourselves publicly defending decisions we had made years earlier, only to be nagged by private regrets. Wait a minute! This was supposed to be fun—a gift! Instead, a maelstrom seemed to be brewing.

"Let Me Have My Joy"

In 1938 a group of researchers from Harvard University set out to answer the question of what habits led to a fulfilling life.

They chose a group of 268 men who for the next seventy-five years were studied on a range of psychological, physical, economic, and spiritual characteristics. Called the Grant Study (named after its patron W. T. Grant, the department-store baron), it became the longest-running longitudinal study of human development. With the remaining participants now reaching into their early nineties, George Vaillant, the last acting director of the Grant Study, decided to bring it to a close by publishing what they had learned in a remarkable book called *Triumphs of Experience*. After more than seventy-five years of research, they learned that while factors such as education, a stable marriage, and healthy lifestyle choices were all helpful for a good life, there was only one thing that really mattered to a vibrant life: love. The capacity to love and be loved is the point of our human existence. "The only thing that really matters in life [is] your relations to other people," Vaillant said.[5]

That's it. Basic. "Love your neighbor as you love yourself" kind of stuff. It

> We are here in order to help others, and when we do that, it brings us joy.

really is all about others. Popular TED speaker Simon Sinek says that this motivation for others is the inherent piece that makes us human. We are here in order to help others, and when we do that, it brings us joy. But it's likely you don't need a TED talk—you've learned this lesson from your own life. That's universal too.

A friend told us how, for him, generosity is forever linked to joy. He had been visiting a subsistence farmer named James Kwame on his place outside Accra, Ghana. After they spent a few hours of walking and working the farm in the heat of the day, the farmer's son brought out some sodas. The price of a Coke in Ghana is roughly $1.50, and a subsistence farmer makes something along the lines of $1,000 per year. For James, those sodas represented several days of wages. You and I would likely call it a sacrifice to serve sodas to strange visitors who happened to just show up. Knowing what this hospitality had cost his host, our friend reached for his wallet as he got up to leave. But the farmer refused to take the money despite all the protests. "Do you want to rob me of my joy?" James asked. "It is for my joy that I give you these things. Please. Let me have my joy."[6]

Some things are so good, you just have to share them.

Please, let me have my joy. Some things are so good, you just have to share them.

Deciding toward Giving

After several weeks of releasing steam, our conversations calmed down, took a different tone. By the time our elder board gathered with our finance committee, nearly everyone agreed that under no circumstances should we use this windfall to shore up a deficit. Our annual budget was just that: a budget that should be met with our annual offerings.

Good. One decision made. But making one decision only led to other decisions. As leaders we felt a responsibility to bat around ideas to present to the congregation. The board knew that constructing a parking lot would take all the money we had and then some. In taking parking off the table, we opened other doors.

We had a number of other very practical needs. Our church treasurer reminded us that a capital campaign a few years earlier had left a $1.3 million mortgage on our ministry building. Wouldn't paying off the mortgage be a good use of the money? And isn't Scripture filled with verses advising us to live debt-free? Paying off the mortgage started to look like not only a fiscally responsible decision, but a *righteous decision* as well. (Conversations can get complicated when we believe righteousness is on the line.)

Fiscal prudence wasn't the only option that had a halo of holiness. We recognized that our windfall was a by-product from a gentrifying neighborhood.

Some argued we had a moral imperative to re-invest in other city neighborhoods where middle- and lower-income families were being pushed out. Related to this was the feeling that because our funds came from a low-income housing investment, the most responsible action was to invest in another housing project. The discussions were heavy. Ponderous. Each one of us feeling the weight to *do this right*.

Suddenly out of the air of responsibility came the wild, counter-intuitive idea to simply begin by giving some of the money away. And not just a token amount either, but to give away $160,000 dollars—10 percent of our amount. In religious language, the 10 percent would be a tithe. Throughout the Bible it was a common practice to give the first 10 percent of one's harvest as an offering to God. Well, we think it's common—but now (perhaps like then), while we may aspire to give away 10 percent, most of us (even those who identify as *very religious*) don't give much more than 3 percent.

How liberating it would be to simply give such a large portion of money away! What a surprising example of grace and freedom it would show the world. Churches are infamous for repeatedly asking for money. But we were in a position to give money. Why not give the first 10 percent *to the people* and ask them to do whatever they thought God wanted them to do with it?

> Churches are infamous for repeatedly asking for money. But we were in a position to give money.

The idea was eagerly presented to the church board and was met by . . . silence. Finally, one member responded, "The church *is* the tithe. We *ask for* money—we don't give it!" Umm, yes. We do ask for money. But what if we didn't? What if we showed the congregation we trusted them to do good with gifts they never sought or expected to receive? In the same way God had trusted all of us by placing this world into the hands of men and women in the first place?

In fact, what if this entire exercise of tithing to the people became a metaphor for what God does for us every single day? In other words, while we would give the gift of "free money" and ask individuals to do something good with it, we would also be pointing to the reality that every one of us has something far more valuable than free money. And that daily we are being asked to do something good with it. We are given a window of time and energy and passion and asked to live to our potential. To do something good with this gift of our "one precious life," as the poet Mary Oliver puts it.

While our meeting started in silence, the longer we discussed the tithe idea, the more excited some people became. Some could see the connection and how it might make God's generosity visible in new ways. They felt like we were actually living the parable of the loaves and the fishes. Others reasoned that the proposed tithe would invite us to see just how many good things are going on in the world around us. Being exposed to the passionate good work of others might allow us to see past the boundaries of our personal projects and interests.

And yet . . . there continued to be a huge pause. This was a new idea. Our bylaws didn't give the board explicit permission to "dispose of church funds" in excess of $25,000, and we were debating disposing of $160,000.

Cue the lawyers.

Very soon we had three of them knee-deep in ecclesiastic regulations. Just what did we mean by "dispose"? If the resources were going to be distributed to the members, could that mean that the money actually stayed in the church and therefore was not "disposed" to an outside party? And did our church bylaws even apply to this situation, since the check had been written to the housing foundation that the church had created decades ago?

Hmmm.

"The letter of the law kills but the Spirit gives life," said the Apostle Paul in his second letter to the Corinth church (2 Cor. 3:6). You can say that again. The purpose of laws is to establish standards, maintain order, and settle disputes. Important things. Necessary things. But outside of a courtroom, laws are not the things that stir our blood and ignite the imaginations of most of us. And if the law fails to inspire us, then the letter of the law must have been the first-century equivalent of being lost in the weeds.

Paul contrasted the crazy explosion Jesus let loose in the

world with the tightly wound girdle of the law. Jesus blurred the lines and challenged the definitions of what the law was even supposed to do. He picked grain on the Sabbath because he and his disciples were hungry. He healed people on the Sabbath because they were sick. Jesus seemed to say the law was created so people could flourish!

As the days crawled forward, it struck us that two thousand years later we were working through something similar. All of our hearts were stirred by the sheer unexpected joy of receiving a sizable check—gratis! But would people value something that was just given to them? Would any of us treat a free gift as carefully as one we had worked to receive?

Our concerns and our hopes were all out on the table. Was it faith or folly to give away $160,000 with no strings attached?

Our first round of voting by the board was inconclusive. A majority wanted to go ahead and give a tithe. But there was enough strong disagreement that it didn't feel like a full vote of confidence. We decided to meet two weeks later, giving people a little more time to pray over the matter, though the delay truly reflected the fact that the discussion was wearing several of us down. The joyful, wonderful whimsy of freely giving to the church had truly stalled under the weight of the bylaws and

> *Our concerns and our hopes were all out on the table. Was it faith or folly to give away $160,000 with no strings attached?*

objections. Time was growing short. Not only did we need to tell the congregation about the Atrium money, but if we were going to gift the tithe, then we needed to do it first thing out of the box. Otherwise it wouldn't really be a tithe.

We set the date for the announcement of the windfall: the first Sunday after Labor Day. But would we be able to release the first $160,000 freely to the people?

A few days before that eventful Sunday, we met one last time. But this time the pastor came in and said we should "table the tithe," just take it out of consideration. There was something more important at stake: unity of love. And while the tithe seemed like the right thing, our strong words and open frustrations threatened to undermine the joy of the entire project. "If we are to learn love through all of this, we're off to a bad start."

Silence . . . again. But a different kind this time. This was the silence of sadness. Of disappointment. Of loss. You never know how badly you wanted to do something until the opportunity is gone. Similarly, we didn't realize how much freedom we felt *with just the idea* of generosity until it was sunk. The weight of the air felt as heavy as our hearts. "It could have been so thrilling!" one board member said. It was then that our conversation started to pivot. Instead of looking for a way to say no, we started exploring how we could say yes. Our focus shifted from trying to explain away the idea to how we could defend it.

After another fifteen minutes of discussion, we asked for a show of hands from those who wanted to say yes. Slowly almost every hand around the table went up. While the vote wasn't unanimous, the spirit was in unison. In four days' time, every one of our congregants would receive a check for five hundred dollars. They would be told: God trusts you to do something good in the world. And so do we.

In four days' time, every one of our congregants would receive a check for five hundred dollars. They would be told: God trusts you to do something good in the world. And so do we.

What is it that happens when people are willing to risk? What emerges when they are willing to let go? Our church discovered just how important each one of us is to this entire enterprise called life. Generosity made us closer friends, better citizens, and more loving souls. This book is our story, but it's really generosity's story, which means it can be your story too.

This book is our story, but it's really generosity's story, which means it can be your story too.

CHAPTER 2

THE PLANE OF GENEROSITY

Scarcity. The word evokes discomfort, deficiency, want. Like an ill-fitting sweater shrunken after a wash, scarcity pinches in all the wrong places and exposes more skin than we like. Scarcity *scares* many of us, and we reflexively tug at its hem and sleeves to slacken its hold.

Ours is a church that knows scarcity. Intimately. Left bankrupt by construction efforts, the Swedish immigrants who built the church in 1886 never once worshiped in it. Eighty years later, the church's monthly bills hung limply from a basement bulletin board, visually begging congregants to fend off the debt collectors. Churchgoers tutored neighborhood children by flashlight to avoid electricity expense.

Despite a history of scarcity, LaSalle Street Church also has maintained an intimate, long-term commitment to generosity. Situated on the near north side of Chicago in a diverse and sometimes volatile neighborhood, LaSalle has a history of getting involved in our community. During Chicago's race riots in the 1960s, the local youth protected the church from burning because it was one of the few institutions they trusted. LaSalle had invested in the neighborhood, from the senior citizens who needed company and a meal, to the kids who sought a safe place to go after school, to the residents caught up in a legal system they couldn't navigate. LaSalle's repeated acts of generosity loosened scarcity's hold. Not that generosity altered the church's financial circumstances. It didn't. But giving changed the way LaSalle wore its scarcity.

Generosity possesses the power to reshape us, whether we frequent a church, synagogue, mosque, yoga studio, or nothing at all. But how do we begin to access generosity's power?

During the season when the church's bills were publicly draped like laundry on the line, the people outside the church's back door faced their own kinds of pressures. Many found themselves caught up in a shifting political tide on the topic of public housing—their own homes included.

Generosity possesses the power to reshape us, whether we frequent a church, synagogue, mosque, yoga studio, or nothing at all.

In the late 1950s and early 1960s, Chicago officials embraced urban renewal, creating high-density, high-rise dwellings like Cabrini-Green. At the time, LaSallers joked that the program would have been more aptly named *urban removal*. The families living in the church's neighboring row houses—people who provided a stabilizing force in the community—confronted the prospect of being re-located to these new developments throughout the city.

During that time, Senior Pastor Bill Leslie preached a commitment to turf. LaSalle's turf has long been along the edges of communities in transition. You've read how ecologists find the greatest biodiversity of plant life along the edge where different habitats join? LaSalle occupied the urban version of that principle. One set of doors welcomed some of our city's neediest residents, while another set of doors opened to some of the most expensive real estate in Chicago. Leslie believed that LaSalle could be a meeting place where everyone was welcomed.

Local congressman Robert L. Thompson worried over the impact of urban renewal on the thousands of constituents facing displacement. A long-time resident and an African-American, he practiced commitment to turf much like Leslie did. When he was offered a bribe of ten thousand dollar to influence the award of rights to the land occupied by LaSalle's row house neighbors, Thompson refused. And then promptly phoned Leslie.

Leslie, he said. *We have to act. Now.*

In the space of two months, Leslie rallied LaSalle and several other churches to invest one thousand dollars each in a campaign to secure land rights. Leslie surely fretted over the amount, considering his own salary hovered around three thousand dollars.[1]

Why does a congregation barely scraping by dig in and

scrape deeper to ensure its neighbors stay put? Because, to quote Reverend D. T. Niles, which Leslie liked to do, "Christianity is one beggar telling another beggar where he found bread." Generosity at LaSalle began the way it begins anywhere: with the recognition that we're all in this *together*. The fifty-some churchgoers at LaSalle saw themselves in their neighbors' faces. They understood their neighbors' struggles as their own struggles too. They knew their neighbors needed them. But they also knew they needed their neighbors.

Scanning the landscape, those beggars of LaSalle Street Church saw a larger context for their decisions. They glimpsed the potential for an answer to their neighbors' housing problems to the west, and understood they played a role in shaping this turf, this plot of terrain juxtaposed against the pristine homes of high society to the east. Literally sitting beneath the shadow of two towers of physical and social structure, LaSalle caught a crack of daylight and decided to follow it. As if surveying an aerial view of the church, the congregation, its neighborhood, and a bigger plan, LaSalle found that pursuit of this light led it to a different plane.

Generosity resides on that plane. Not hard or heroic, generosity at LaSalle simply began with awareness. This is how generosity always begins. Every day, even when squeezed by scarcity, we receive opportunities to view the world from the vantage point of generosity. Generosity reorients us to others and to our own contexts. Generosity allows us to step boldly and humbly into a greater narrative where our actions move the plot forward. Generosity grants us the freedom and perspective to be the beggar telling another beggar where to find food.

Whereas scarcity likes to command our attention. We can't help looking at its sweater, barely tolerating its discomfort, longing for a different garment. Generosity, however, draws our gaze away— and into a larger story of abundance.

> *Generosity allows us to step boldly and humbly into a greater narrative where our actions move the plot forward.*

A Matter of Scale

The brilliant psychologist Daniel Kahneman (brilliant being no exaggeration: he is a *psychologist* who won a Nobel Prize in *economics*) uses the acronym WYSIATI for "What you see is all there is."[2] Our lightning-fast brains, he says, excel at creating a consistent story from the data and observations we have at hand. The downside of this almost immediate story-creating? We ignore crucial information, simply because its discovery necessitates effort. If we can construct a logical story from the information we have, why bother seeking out new facts, figures, or ideas?

Much of the time our logical stories serve us well. The

human race has long depended on the rapid conclusions we draw: our predecessors wouldn't stop to ask each other if they might have missed relevant data when they sensed a predator crouched behind foliage. The decision to flee paid off most of the time . . . except when the animal cowering behind the bush had taken cover from a carnivorous creature opposite the plain, precisely where our primitive ancestors sought escape.

In modern times, ignoring relevant data rarely results in life-or-death consequences. But neither is it inconsequential. Today, when what we see is all there is, we no longer risk death. But we do risk missing a meaningful life when we choose *just living*.

Our penchant for making observations and drawing rapid conclusions starts early. From a young age, we learn that money doesn't grow on trees, money makes the world go round, a dollar saved is a dollar earned, and, by golly, you get what you pay for! We learn about survival of the fittest and picking ourselves up by the bootstraps. We learn that love proves fickle, resources are scarce, and opportunities come few and far between.

Yet what we see is *not* all there is.

What if we sought to perceive *all* the data? What if we corrected the distortions caused by the imperfect human systems ordering our world? What if we resided on the plane of generosity, grasping the entirety of the vision the Creator had in the first place, not just what we see in front of us? Would we no longer settle for *just living*?

We have a long legacy of ancestors who share our myopia, our tendency to observe narrowly. You've probably heard the parable of the blind men and the elephant. In the story a number of blind men gather around an elephant, touch a particular part of it, and then describe what stands before them.

What if we resided on the plane of generosity, grasping the entirety of the vision the Creator had in the first place, not just what we see in front of us?

While versions of the parable appear in Hindu, Sufi, and Jain texts, perhaps the oldest version dates from Buddhist writings. In this account, one blind man touches the ear, one the tusk, another the trunk, and others the foot, back, tail, and tuft of the tail. Predictably, each blind man describes the elephant differently, convinced of the others' mistakes in judgment. The parable as written in the Buddhist Udana concludes with the raja comparing the blind men to the religious leaders of the day:

> "Just so are these preachers and scholars holding various views blind and unseeing. . . . In their ignorance they are by nature quarrelsome, wrangling, and disputatious, each maintaining reality is thus and thus."

Then the Exalted One rendered this meaning by uttering this verse of uplift:

> *O how they cling and wrangle, some who claim*
> *For preacher and monk the honored name!*

For, quarreling, each to his view they cling.

Such folk see only one side of a thing.[3]

Even those admired leaders, the "preachers and scholars," failed to see the whole. But perhaps most unsettling in the parable is that each blind man described, *with complete accuracy*, what he felt when he touched the elephant. Not one erred in observation, analysis, or description. Their failure had nothing to do with misunderstanding what appeared in front of them. Their failure came in knowing only part of the truth, not the whole truth. Somehow they missed the test instructions directing them to take a few steps, touch again, and repeat. And in dismissing the others' observations, they sacrificed an opening for knowledge, a drawing back of the curtain shading the window of wisdom.

Some of our ancestors *could* see the bigger picture, redirecting their gazes to view the larger arc of our universal story, the meta-narrative in which their smaller stories resided. They scaled up, even when the circumstances might have justified burying their heads in the sand—as in Job's case.

Both Christians and Jews recognize the story of Job. The Old Testament devotes an entire chapter to this man who is a riches-to-rags-to-riches story. The scene opens with Job at the top of his game, with a happy family, a healthy spiritual life, immense wealth, and much fame, enough to merit the label "the greatest of all the people of the east" (Job 1:3). But a few verses later, Satan enters. He dishes up some trash talk with God, suggesting Job only obeys God because Job's blessings abound.

Just a fair-weather fan, you
envision Satan goading. *Let
me prove it to you.* God permits Satan to overturn Job's
fortunes: Job's children die,
his belongings fall to ruin—
even his body betrays him as
his skin erupts in sores. Yet

Some of our ancestors could see the bigger picture, redirecting their gazes to view the larger arc of our universal story.

Job continues to profess his faith in God—even falling to the ground to worship.

Most of us construe Job's story as a lesson about faith. Job remains faithful, far more faithful than any of us might be on a good day, in fact. But his story also instructs us on perspective. Job trains his vision on God, not himself. Job looks beyond his own reflection in the mirror. Maybe because Job's demise occurs rapidly, maybe because his body offends all of their senses, Job's friends who come to console him limit their sight to the outlines of their mirrors. Would we behave any differently?

These friends interpret Job's suffering as divine punishment for sin. Indeed, most of the book of Job consists of the friends in a pattern of dialogue with Job. *Fess up and ask forgiveness!* they implore, to which Job pleads innocence. Then the friends repeat their petition: *Look deeper—you must have missed something!*

Though these friends speak at length of God and God's role

in this drama, they focus on Job as the main character in the story. They only see what is right in front of them: this formerly mighty man reduced to a destitute, blistered, inhuman-looking human. Given what religious men preached at the time, their logic seems sound. They cannot conceive of any different framework outside the one they created: sin causes suffering; Job is suffering; therefore, Job sinned.

Job knew that the wisest people of his day would have backed his friends in the debate. But Job also knew something even more profound: somehow, some way, this story eclipsed him. Though the elephant's tusk would have been easy to focus on, Job yearned to understand the whole beast. Experiencing suffering like Job's, most of us would opt to see the world darkly, to focus on all that was lost. But Job turned his gaze away and upward. He knew what he saw was not all there was.

When the state congressman approached Bill Leslie, LaSalle heard an invitation to participate in a larger narrative about the neighborhood. The church had other worthy ways to use the money. In addition to having bills to pay, LaSalle had nascent ministries—a tutoring program for the kids who lived in Cabrini-Green, a weekly meal and fellowship time for the elderly in the neighborhood, and the first Christian legal-aid clinic in the nation—that needed financial support.

An outsider would have looked at LaSalle in 1970 and seen a church that could barely pay its bills, with ministries operating in survival mode, and a population of increasingly needy people living within earshot of the church's bells. It's not hard to imagine people wondering if funding the housing project risked LaSalle's ability to meet critical needs just beyond its sanctuary door. A pragmatist might have argued for investing a dollar in the congregants leading the new ministries, presuming it to generate a more certain return than a dollar in a speculative housing endeavor. How many of us might have said, wistfully but assuredly, now is not the time?

All visible signs pointed in the direction of turning away from the housing effort and focusing heads-down on LaSalle's challenges inside its walls. But generosity challenges us to lift up our heads and to scan the horizon. Generosity asks us to *defy* our tendency toward WYSIATI, as Job did and as the small congregation at LaSalle sought to do.

Experiencing suffering like Job's, most of us would opt to see the world darkly, to focus on all that was lost. But Job turned his gaze away and upward. He knew what he saw was not all there was.

Redirecting Our Gaze

Our realism, our pragmatism, and our rootedness in the visible handicap our ability to grasp the bigger picture. Concentrating on the reflection in the mirror, we dismiss everything outside the frame.

Across cultures and across time, people have identified with the objects around them. From Paleolithic man with his rudimentary tools, to modern-day Americans and the 300,000 objects in their homes, we humans invest a portion of our identity into the stuff of our lives and interpret our world through these objects.[4] Our objects contain meaning. But trusting our identity to objects leaves us vulnerable. Do these symbols of ourselves command our attention to the extent that we cannot look away? Do we view money as the ultimate container, because its fungibility allows it to adopt any symbol or representation we desire?

If so, our containers have forfeited life outside the container.

The story of generosity begins with redirecting our gaze. We unlock eyes with the reflection of scarcity staring back at us from the mirror. We retreat from the magnetic pull of the

Our realism, our pragmatism, and our rootedness in the visible handicap our ability to grasp the bigger picture.

objects in the looking glass. Generosity takes us outside the frame, revealing a backdrop of grand and gorgeous proportions. When we shift our perspective from the two-dimensional mirror to the three-dimensional world outside the frame, generosity alters the picture.

Ironically, we begin to shift our gaze only when we notice our containers binding and blinding us, and we *accept* our investment in objects. When we take stock of our containers and objects and begin to *give them away*, we shift the nature of our relationship with those things. The act of giving disarms the power that objects hold over us. Our church witnessed that disarming power eight thousand miles away, in a village in Tanzania where dozens of our church members sponsor children.

The story of generosity begins with redirecting our gaze.

In 2011, approximately 23.5 million people in sub-Saharan Africa were HIV positive, totaling almost 70 percent of the global HIV-infected population. Even after the infusion of major aid dollars and tremendous progress on prevention, 1.2 million sub-Saharan Africans died from AIDS that year.[5]

In Tanzania specifically, 5 percent of the population lived with HIV/AIDS in 2011.[6] Eleven percent of all Tanzanian children were orphaned, where at least one parent had died from HIV.[7] Orphaned children fended for themselves, becoming heads of households at very young ages. Luckier children found extended family members to care for them.

When a small group of LaSallers traveled to a remote village outside Arusha, Tanzania, we met a soft-spoken young
woman named Laura Thomas (in Swahili, pronounced La-
OOH-ra). In her mud-and-thatch hut set on a barren dirt landscape, she was raising fourteen children, some of whom were
her own, while others had been orphaned and entrusted to her.
Laura herself carried an HIV-positive diagnosis. Her husband,
the father of all these children, had fallen victim to AIDS. Laura
had landed in a seemingly impossible scenario.

Yet when we met Laura and the children, every one of
those fourteen children was healthy and well-nourished. All
but the youngest attended school. Perched side by side along
a narrow wooden bench, they smiled and giggled, clothed in
their tidy navy-blue school uniforms. We met Laura by way of
World Vision, as her family received support through its program for orphans and vulnerable children. But Laura and her
family's support included another benefactor: her neighbor.

Had we not been told of this neighbor, there is no way we
would have known of his existence. The word "neighbor" has
a loose definition in the Tanzanian countryside. Often, a neighbor lives out of visual range, several kilometers away. From
Laura's house, you couldn't spot a nearby dwelling. But Laura
did have a neighbor—a middle-aged Tanzanian man.

After Laura's husband died, this gentleman visited regularly, bringing food each time and inquiring about the family's
needs. He shared gifts of food and money, and he had given of

himself, as evidenced by the children who called him "uncle" despite the absence of any blood relation. No obligation or rational reason explained his support. At the time, according to the World Bank, the Tanzanian GDP per capita amounted to 504 U.S. dollars. In remote villages like Laura's, families found themselves fortunate to command a fraction of such income. Her neighbor was not giving from his plenty. He was simply giving. Laura's neighbor lived like a beggar showing another beggar where to find bread.

Laura's neighbor did not amass belongings to distinguish himself from others. He did not believe in a zero-sum world where her increase meant his decrease. He did not view his possessions in the context of a story of scarcity. He did not limit his conclusions to what faced him each day upon opening the door of his hut: a chronically impoverished community with frequent droughts and not enough food to sustain it. Instead, he invested himself in objects he gave away freely. He allowed those objects to define him as a giver.

Laura's neighbor envisioned a different story unfolding. He could imagine the plotline leading to Laura's survival, the education and growth of her children, a future awash in love and hope and community. He saw past his story in an effort to see a bigger story.

When we meet the face of suffering, what strikes us first? Do we focus on intractable problems perpetuated by unjust systems, rooted in the ugly muck of the human condition? Do we assume ourselves impotent to address suffering so vast and entrenched?

Psychologist Kahneman admits his pessimism about our natural tendencies to rely only on what we see. In order to formulate consistent narratives, he says, we will *intentionally avoid* seeing more than what there is and ignore new data that may be introduced. In certain situations, however, we actively seek data we do not have, Kahneman notes. For example, when purchasing a home, we methodically gather information about comparable houses, neighborhood characteristics, and school district reports. We hire inspectors to check behind walls, to understand structural strengths and weaknesses, to find potential threats to the proper functioning of the various systems within a house. While we initially notice only the charming curbside appeal of a home, we acknowledge our need to incorporate additional factors into our decision.

Buying a home is a big decision, but it's not the biggest decision of our lives. If we fail to re-orient our vision, what do we risk? Our own stories and, perhaps more importantly, the bigger story in draft form by the Creator. But when we intentionally expand our narrow frames, we view the world anew.

Our culture teaches us to focus on the confining boundaries of scarcity. Remember those axioms repeated since our youth about money not growing on trees and tightening our belts and stretching every dollar? Yet the Creator designed us as generous people.

The Chicago Orleans Housing Corporation (COHC) incorporated on November 24, 1970. This partnership of churches shared a straightforward mission: to secure the land rights in order to ensure families stayed in the neighborhood. A simple mission, but an incredibly complicated task. The parcel of land across the street appraised at *ten million* dollars. The bribe offered to the state representative more than doubled the total investment of the churches!

If we fail to re-orient our vision, what do we risk? Our own stories and, perhaps more importantly, the bigger story in draft form by the Creator. But when we intentionally expand our narrow frames, we view the world anew.

For three years, the church partnership negotiated with the Department of Urban Renewal to obtain the land rights. After finally receiving the department's endorsement, COHC ran head on into an eighteen-month moratorium on the granting of federal housing funds. Securing a construction loan absorbed another five years of the churches' time. But they stayed true to their mission and their task.

Atrium Village broke ground in 1976, and by 1979 the first residents settled in. "It was an experiment without a precedent," former pastor Bruce Otto recounted years later. "No one knew if the project would last the first four years, much less the next forty." Not only did Atrium Village last—it flourished.

CHAPTER 3

ABUNDANCE, NOT SCARCITY

We were born to tell stories. Stories of tall tales and heroic conquests; tearful narratives of lost love and never-ending stories of slightly exaggerated truths. And we tell them all. Stories are how we make sense of our lives and our place in the world. Stories make sense of our random activities; they describe someone's outrageous conduct and how we made up, or set it right, or decided, *Never again!*

In our stories we can steal the spotlight and do the star turn or take the humble bow. We can be whoever we want to be or wish we could be. And this is important because research reveals that *we become the stories we tell*. If you repeat a story often enough, it will become a kind of established truth. You probably have a few stories that you've told so often for

Research reveals that we become the stories we tell.

so long that they've become part of the furniture of your life. Perhaps the story of how you met your life partner or how you got to where you are in your work. You've likely drawn some lessons from these stories. Lessons you've shared with others in an effort to teach them the truth you've learned.

We're here to tell you that some of the stories we have heard and told throughout our lives were simply wrong. We didn't know they were wrong—we thought we were just telling it like it is. But the stories we were telling weren't the whole truth.

We're here to tell you that some of the stories we have heard and told throughout our lives were simply wrong.

We told stories of fear when there was actually more hope than fear at work. We told stories of individualism when actually there was a cast of characters. We told stories of stinginess when abundance was all around. We told the partial stories because we hadn't stepped back to seek an account of the bigger picture of all that was around us.

Stephen Jay Gould was one of the twentieth century's most influential biologists. Gould is remembered for forcing some of the fiercest debates in evolutionary biology in part because he took on the assumptions and the stories that had been received as accepted truth. He operated under the belief that "the most erroneous stories are the ones we think we know best—and therefore never scrutinize or question."

From the beginning Atrium Village challenged the assumptions and predictions that policymakers had pronounced upon the urban poor. Atrium Village (unimaginatively named for the nine-story open atrium dominating the first apartment tower) was the first housing development in the country to be financed and constructed by state, private, and church funding. This was a housing development embodying a larger narrative which declared that in a city marked by clear divisions of race and income, people of different ethnicities and incomes could live together. It took years before all the players finally agreed to the vision of a truly diverse project: 50 percent black and 50 percent white; 50 percent market rate and 50 percent under-market rate rents.

"The most erroneous stories are the ones we think we know best—and therefore never scrutinize or question."

And everyone was worried about something.

People feared that the balanced ratio of whites and blacks would not hold. The market-rate tenants worried about the property getting run down. The under-market folks wondered if they would be accepted. And everyone—developers, residents, and church leaders—worried about safety. This was, after all, an area where drivers wrapped and padlocked heavy chains around their car hoods to keep their batteries from being stolen while they were at work. Petty crime and more serious assaults were typical.

As far as possible, those designing the development tried to lessen the fear factor: the central atrium left no dark hallways, the glass elevators allowed light and visibility, and the courtyard area around the buildings provided safe spaces for children to play.

Atrium Village opened to a flood of three thousand applications. The fears didn't come to pass—or most of them, at least. A newly minted church intern was sexually assaulted shortly after moving in. We were sickened and angry; years later that memory continues to sting. But on the whole Atrium was so safe, well- maintained, and well-managed that thirty-five years later, some of the original residents were still happily living in their units. Atrium Village proved to be not only a solid anchor in the community but also a standard bearer for community-based best practices in housing.

Atrium Village questioned the prevailing narrative. It was the first of three building projects LaSalle undertook in the neighborhood. All of them focused on building community engagement among people who were different from one another.

Framing Stories

Building Atrium Village wasn't a one-off decision. Instead, it was a deliberate choice to write another chapter in the book of abundance.

If you've heard the term *framing story*, you'll know that it refers to the grand story narrative that helps explain all the other stories that follow it. Like a set of nesting dolls that opens one to the next, each tale that comes after the framing story carries the carved characteristics of her predecessors. When four churches on the north side of Chicago came together to build a housing development, they weren't just operating from the stories they had told and lived throughout the years. They were also pointing back to a framing story that said something about their very identity.

The Judeo-Christian narrative opens with a whopper of a framing story: a faceless, nameless God intentionally creates a world of beauty, diversity, and wonder. It was a fragile, cosmic world of moving planets, cycles of life and death, expanding space, and continually unfolding mysteries. This world contained tiny elements of elaborate invisible beauty *(snowflakes!)*, a seemingly endless array of species *(twelve thousand different ant species alone!)*, and awe-producing glory *(the Grand Tetons!)*.

> *Like a set of nesting dolls that opens one to the next, each tale that comes after the framing story carries the carved characteristics of her predecessors.*

This God created everything wonderful and good. And then, in one swift move, this same God handed it over to men and women. *To the creatures!* Those twelve thousand ant species? Their destiny was now controlled by the sons of Adam. The mountain ranges of Wyoming? Their fate was up to Eve.

From the naming of the animals to the tilling of the ground, all the beauty and wonder was given to us: you, me, and the guy down the street. The livelihood of creation was entrusted to us. We were asked to treat it carefully and love it well. We were invited to help the earth and humankind flourish together. Our very first framing story is the story of a generous God who freely yields everything to us. There was enough for the earth to flourish and for people to prosper. We were invited to take part in a very good world.

Leaning into this framing story has all sorts of implications for how human life is constructed. It means that before we were gripped by the fear of scarcity, we knew the reality of abundance; before we felt the spasm of self-protection, we felt the pleasure of plenty.

> Our very first framing story is the story of a generous God who freely yields everything to us.

And before there was a story of human isolation and fear, there was a bigger and greater story of community and blessing.

But would people remember it?

In the early 2000s, almost twenty-five years after Atrium opened, LaSalle got word that the primary investor in the development wanted to sell its interest. The restrictive covenants on Atrium would soon expire without the possibility of renewal. The city of Chicago was in the throes of demolishing Cabrini-Green, the public-housing complex that had been a long-time neighborhood fixture. A new policy study from the University of Chicago was advocating that the best way of tackling intransigent poverty was to provide communities where people of different incomes could live together. Exactly what Atrium's vision had been decades earlier. Now the Chicago public-housing authority was going to try to implement that vision on a large scale.

Leaning into this framing story has all sorts of implications for how human life is constructed. It means that before we were gripped by the fear of scarcity, we knew the reality of abundance.

A model called "scat-tered site" housing was trans-forming monolithic housing columns throughout Chicago into lower-density, low-rise units serving diverse populations. At Monday-morning staff meetings at our church, we sat and watched the thirty-story Cabrini buildings fall to the ground. We listened while long-time residents told stories about the life they had loved before the gangs and drug lords took control, and we said good-bye to families who bravely moved to new neighborhoods throughout Chicago.

We were excited for the possibilities some would have, but we were also witnessing a neighborhood decidedly changing. Retail developers eyed the newly vacant land. Condominiums costing upwards of half a million dollars were being planned, and churches like LaSalle who framed their ministry on being bridge churches were trying to determine what it meant to have a commitment to a neighborhood that was rapidly disappearing.

These were the concerns around the table when church leaders got together to discuss the possibility of a sale. While the churches owned only a 15 percent interest in Atrium Village, our voting bloc could stop the sale of the development. What we couldn't do was force new restrictions to be placed on the property after the old ones expired. And without some sort of requirement for low-income ratios, the housing development would almost certainly be exclusively market-rate.

Two of the partner churches located in the middle of Cabrini were down to just handfuls of congregants. Their membership had suffered such steep declines that they faced almost certain closure by their denominations. They advocated selling—quickly—while negotiating with the city and the future owners to obtain an equal or greater number of set-aside units. Others weren't so sure. While the overall number of low-income units might be higher, the percentage of such units in the new complex would be reduced. Were we abandoning our mission and our principles by selling? Were there some other possibilities we hadn't yet seen? As the discussions continued, the churches each committed their next steps to prayer and reflection.

At LaSalle Street Church, this reflection included some strong discussions not only about whether we should sell, but what was the most responsible thing to do with any money we might receive from a proposed sale. As many leaders saw it, we had one challenge: parking. Over the previous year we had lost all Sunday-morning parking options in our immediate neighborhood. With the sale of Atrium, we were going to lose our mid-week parking as well.

Parking was a real need, and lack of parking was a real fear. But how much weight should we give this need? And how much should we feed this fear? We didn't want our parking worries to cloud our judgment . . . but still, *could we exist without a parking lot?*

> There's always some nagging fear that stands in the way of operating freely. When that fear arises, we are called to remember our framing story.

There's always some nagging fear that stands in the way of operating freely. When that fear arises, we are called to remember our framing story. So we at LaSalle began to recall some of the ways we had stepped out in faith, trusting the generous nature of God. The initial Atrium investment, the construction of a building for senior housing, the birth of a legal-aid clinic—all of these were initiated because of the conviction that we lived in a world where there was *more than enough* to do the work we were called to do.

The stories of the Old and New Testament have the ability to draw people's attention back—over and over again—to the essential reality of an abundant world. From Abraham to Moses, and from Jonah to Jesus, God keeps pushing us to experience the fullness of the abundant world. The results are decidedly mixed.

Perhaps the first man who really got this message was the lonely figure of Abraham. Abraham appears in a region marked by warring tribes and a shortage of water.

Without being given much explanation, Abraham not only understood the fundamental principle of God's abundance; he built his entire life around this framing story. Abraham is perhaps the first man in whom we see both the fullness of generosity coupled with the lingering threads of fear that mark so many of us.

Readers beginning the story know just the bare facts. Abraham is the oldest son of three. When his younger brother dies early, he leaves his son, Lot, in Abraham's care. Then Abraham follows his father toward the land of Canaan, but they never arrive. Terah dies in Haran, a town in present-day Syria. It is here—when Abraham is living in a foreign land, absorbing the loss of his father, and finding himself saddled with a nephew who will be a source of great pain (perhaps Abraham already has inklings of that future)—that God offers Abraham a new way of seeing the world. And gives him the choice to believe or not.

We don't know how the insight comes to Abraham. The text in Genesis 12:1–3 simply says that God found him, addressed him by name, and called him out to a world beyond his immediate worries and insecurities, a world beyond the small frames of his existence to date.

> Leave your country, your people and your father's household and go to the land I will show you. I will make you into a great nation and I will bless you; I will make your name great, and you will be a blessing.

In other words: Don't be afraid, Abraham. There will always be more than enough for you. Your future, your goods, your family—all are in my hands. *And all will be well. There will always be enough.*

Trusting God's promise of abundance will be an ongoing decision. Again and again Abraham will have to fight back fear in order to live into the framing story God has given him. One particularly pronounced encounter comes in the very next chapter of Genesis, when Abraham and his nephew arrive at what will be their final home on the hills of the Negev in what is now southern Israel. Between the two of them they have so much stuff that the land simply can't sustain their combined cattle, sheep, and people. The time has come for them to sep-

Trusting God's promise of abundance will be an ongoing decision.

arate. Abraham takes Lot to a mountain where they can look out over an expansive valley. From this vantage point they can choose the property on which they will settle. Or at least one of them can.

The choices are stark. To the east lies the green valley of the Jordan River (much wider then than it is today), while the west is dominated by the dusty brown hills of southern Canaan. By dint of custom, tradition, and respect, Abraham should be the one to decide where he wants to live, leaving the leftovers to his nephew. It is Abraham's right to choose first. But instead, Abraham turns to Lot and says, "After you."

Not surprisingly, Lot chooses the valley, the one the text says is "well watered, like the garden of the LORD, like the land of Egypt" (Gen. 13:10). Without any further comment or remorse, the men part ways, and Abraham settles into a region that by all appearances is harsher, tougher, and more dangerous than God's grand promise of abundance would suggest it should be.

Sometimes we have to doggedly, determinedly believe what God promised: *There will always be enough.* This is what Abraham shows us. There is enough even when the circumstances aren't what we would have chosen. Even when we're given a "raw deal" or are forced to play a "rotten hand." Abraham was free enough to realize that "What you see is *not* all there is."

The message Abraham learned is one that many people in the world are literally dying to hear. If you and I could believe we have more than enough, then we could pressure our leaders to engage more fully with the remaining pockets of extreme poverty. Since 1990, more than one billion people have risen from the ranks of those living on less than two dollars a day. That is genuine progress to celebrate! A child born today in the majority world is more than twice as likely to live to adolescence, and the overall literacy rate among fifteen- to twenty-four-year-olds has risen to 91 percent.[1]

But this real progress remains tenuous, as shifting weather patterns, fragile local governments, and separatist violence continue to erupt, effectively erasing the incremental gains. Closing the gap *for real* will need the kind of long-term stability that is accomplished only when leaders around the world commit themselves to increasing food security and education, supporting economic growth, and strengthening the mechanisms of accountability and civil institutions—all aspirations that require less fear and more cooperation. All are goals that can be realized if our framing story is rooted in abundance.

But we keep getting stuck.

Abraham occasionally got stuck too. Not long after his shining-faith moment on the mountain, he passes through the foreign land of Gerar. He's worried about his own well-being as well as that of his lovely wife, Sarah. After all, he reasons, "These strangers don't fear the same God I fear; they don't play by the same rules or have the same values I have."

Fear made a fool out of Abraham. In an effort to protect

himself, he bribes the local leader to treat him fairly by offering the most valuable resource he has: his wife.

This is a low point for the righteous Abraham. Sarah is spared violation—but not because her husband finds his courage. Rather, the "scary stranger" in this case, the local leader known as Abimelech, turns out to have a stronger moral code than the mighty Abraham in that moment. Not only does the foreign leader refuse to violate Sarah, but the leader's carefully worded critique to Abraham holds a mirror up to the patriarch's fear: *Remember your framing story, Abraham! You can trust there is enough for all you need.*

Here's the thing about fear: it causes us to focus on what we don't know instead of what we do. It invites us to dwell on the worst of our imaginings and urges us to sum up all the what-ifs. And the thing is, you can't prove fear wrong—there simply aren't enough facts to definitively shut it down. We're never going to be free of fear. But that doesn't mean we have to be paralyzed by it.

We can tell a different story.

Abraham, in a strange land with strange people, is blindsided by his fear over physical safety. Politicians suspiciously eye their opposition. Parents view the shifting tide of culture and social media with nervous incomprehension. And four ur-

We're never going to be free of fear. But that doesn't mean we have to be paralyzed by it. We can tell a different story.

ban pastors apprehensively discuss whether their churches will survive a changing neighborhood. Yet the question for each of them is the same: What story am I going to tell?

Blessed to Be a Blessing

Throughout the Bible there is a push-pull relationship between wealth and want. There are stories about how wealth is a sign of God's favor followed by stories about the dangers of wealth along with the implication that no one should have more than they need. Jesus doesn't solve this debate, either. To one person, Jesus applauds the actions of the wealthy who give generously; to another, Jesus forcefully demands that the rich man sell everything he has.

Yet in the next scene, it appears that Jesus's disciples are receiving resources and assistance from wealthy women who are supportive of his message. Joseph of Arimathea was a well-known supporter who was not only wealthy but provided the grave for Jesus's burial. Clearly those who had some financial resources to give assisted the proclamation of the good news during Jesus's life and in the early church as well.

The apostle Paul often writes about the financial needs of the various church communities of the first century. Paul sees our resources through a very pragmatic focus: those who have must give to those who don't have. "It is a question of a fair balance," he writes to the Corinthian church in seeking support for the church in Jerusalem. "Your surplus is for their need, and their need is for your surplus" (2 Cor. 8:13–14). It's not a coincidence that some have money while others have needs. This is how God's economy works, Paul seems to suggest. We are all here at this particular time because there are ties between us. We all share a connection, a common bond we have one to another, and we complete that bond when we share what we have with one another—needs are offered to those with resources, while those with resources give to the needs. And when that intersection happens, there is an eruption of joy. Of celebration. There is a sense that *this is what we were made for.*

> We all share a connection, a common bond we have one to another, and we complete that bond when we share what we have with one another.

Shane Claiborne, one of the founders and leaders of a Christian community in Philadelphia called The Simple Way, spent several years working with children alongside Mother Teresa in Calcutta, India. One of the best examples of God's economy of abundance comes in the lesson he learned from a homeless eight-year-old boy.

Every week we would throw a party for the street kids, kids 8-10 years old who were homeless, begging all day to survive. Each Tuesday we would get about 100 of them together and throw a party, play games, eat a big meal. One week, one of the kids I had grown close to told me it was his birthday. So I got him an ice cream. He was so excited he stared at it, mesmerized. I have no idea how long it had been since he had eaten ice cream. But what he did next was brilliant. He yelled at all the other kids and told them to come over. He lined them up and gave them all a lick. His instinct was: this is so good I can't keep it for myself. In the end, that's what this whole idea of generosity is all about. Not guilt. It's about the joy of sharing. It's about realizing the good things in life—like ice cream—are too good to keep for ourselves.[2]

Far more destitute economically than likely any of us will ever be, that boy framed his existence as if there was enough for everyone. He had a sense of fullness even in the midst of seemingly crippling scarcity. That's the abundant heart of a child created by a God of abundance.

Stepping into Joy

It was late in the evening by the time of the vote on Atrium's sale. We knew what was at stake. All who had wanted to speak had done so. We understood we were not of one mind. Yet when all the votes were in, it was clear that the way forward was for the churches to sell their interest while negotiating hard for more units set aside for the working poor. Fortunately, the Chicago city tax assessor, our local alderman, and various community groups also supported that initiative. Any redevelopment plan would need to have 20 percent of its units available at below-market rate. It wasn't long after the vote when we received the various appraisals calculating the worth of the upcoming sale. The churches stood to get between 1.5 and 2 million dollars each.

"Wonderful news!" one church board member exclaimed. "Let's build a parking garage!" Then he started to laugh. We all did. By this point we had started to understand that our framing story was one of blessing and giving. While we weren't sure about what we'd do with the windfall, we knew our first step needed to be one that wasn't held hostage to fear. It had to be a step shining with freedom and abundance. A step that would bring us closer to others and make more visible the bonds of hope and love between us.

By this point we had started to understand that our framing story was one of blessing and giving. While we weren't sure about what we'd do with the windfall, we knew our first step needed to be one that wasn't held hostage to fear.

The Sunday morning of the giveaway, a few of us walked into church with rapidly beating hearts and sweaty palms. Outside of the board and our office staff, no one knew what we were about to do. The possibility that we would be seen as squandering $160,000 was a haunting thought. We had no way of knowing how the announcement would be received, and the experience with the church board had shown that it would likely be mixed and perhaps even divisive.

Here we were in the first Sunday of the fall season. The church was crowded and filled with a somewhat expectant air, since we had sent emails out to the congregation urging as many as possible to be in worship that morning but without telling them the reason why.

The sermon text for that morning concerned a story Jesus had told about a king who went away on a long trip, leaving his trusted servants in charge. Each servant had received a certain amount of money and was told to do the king's business while he was gone. The pastor talked about what it had meant for LaSalle Street Church to be doing the king's business for the past several decades. She announced that one piece of that work, Atrium Village, had been sold earlier in the summer and that the four investing churches had each received a check for close to $1.6 million. (There were several gasps throughout the sanctuary. The big number was a surprise.) Together the church would decide what kind of ministry we were called to do with the money. But the church board also wanted each church member to share in the joy of trust and giving right away! After all, it wasn't only "The Church" that had been entrusted with the Master's resources; it was individuals—Susan and Bob and Catrice. And each one of them had a $500 check waiting for them at a lunch following the service. There was food for all! The church was paying for it!

For a few moments, men and women, children and all, just sat in silence. There were no smiles. No high-fives. Just silence.

It started to sink in. Each one of us had something fantastic to give. And we were all going to be giving together.

So the pastor repeated the announcement: "Atrium Village has sold, LaSalle Street Church received a check for $1.6 million, and each one of you has a $500 check waiting for you at lunch!"

That's when the floodgates opened. Some people started to cry. Many started to laugh, and a few stood up and yelled "Hallelujah!"

It started to sink in. Each one of us had something fantastic to give. And we were all going to be giving together—to our neighbors in need, to causes and ministries in a city that we love, and to a world that was then in the throes of the Ebola scare.

Our congregation would enter into a nine-month period of prayer and reflection on what we should do with the remaining money of $1.4 million. But for right now, we would take this step into generosity and joy.

II

STUMBLING TOWARD GENEROSITY

CHAPTER 4

IDENTITY INTACT

The well-loved movie and long-running musical *The Lion King* pivots on a mantra proclaimed by the main character's father: *Remember who you are.*

It's a long-running theme in the literary world, from the ancient figures of *The Odyssey* to Wilbur, the beloved pig of *Charlotte's Web*. Remembering who we are poses a challenge not just to people (and animals) in the fictional world; the theme speaks to us because we find ourselves asking similar questions of identity: Who am I? What's important to me? How am I supposed to live my life?

Remember who you are.

Our big questions can go unanswered or unacknowledged amid the many pressing, very *real* questions commanding our attention, like "What happens if I lose my job?" and "How should I help my aging parents?" Or, in LaSalle's case, "How do we allocate $1.4 million?" and "Where will I spend my $500?"

To answer either question well, we needed to remember

who we were. To explore ourselves deeply and reflectively, to rediscover what we offered and how we might add our signatures to the book of generosity.

Singing Generosity's Tune

On a Friday in July of 2007, fourteen-year-old LaSaller David Melia stumbled upon people giving away hugs outside a movie theater. *Strange*, he thought, and refused to take them up on their offer. Hours later, as the idea bounced back and forth like a pinball in his mind, he found himself intrigued. The next day, David walked Michigan Avenue in downtown Chicago (where nothing comes free!) dispensing hugs while sporting a t-shirt with the words FREE HUGS applied in neon-colored duct tape.

Hugging hooked David. Every day since his first foray on Michigan Avenue, David has worn the words FREE HUGS somewhere on his person—on his shirt, his sleeve, even his forehead. In 2013, as a business management major at DePaul University, David published a book on his experience as a "free hugger" and with the proceeds traveled the following summer to thirteen cities, logging 2,500 hugs on the tour.

David has no question about who he is. He's a serious student, a beloved son, a supportive brother, and a humble Christian. But at his core, David is a hugger. "I am making sure my actions reflect what I believe," noted David. "What I do with my finances, what I want to do as a career, who I spend time with, where I spend my time: those are all resources that I have control over and can use to effect change. There is something in that small act of a hug, in that small gesture, which allows someone to switch their focus from negative to positive. I truly believe small, random acts of kindness have a big effect."

The cynical side of us might retort: *C'mon! At twenty-one, David hasn't experienced the complexities of life; he doesn't have kids or a mortgage or aging parents to support. He's free to be himself.*

True. But David sees a through line in his story that many of us miss. David has connected the various pieces of his journey into an arc of meaning. What if we did something similar? What if we remembered that openness, graciousness, *generosity* once came easily to us?

What if we remembered that openness, graciousness, generosity once came easily to us?

Many of us sense that we once knew generosity well. Generosity feels familiar, and stories like David's remind us of its formerly easy companionship. We recall the language of generosity, the same way the melody of an old song triggers the memory of its lyrics.

When our church treasurer handed out the $500 checks, one by one, under the fluorescent lights of our nondescript fellowship hall, congregants remembered. They remembered when sharing had been part of who they were. They remembered the fun of giving—not because you had to, or got something in return for it, but just because you had something to give. They remembered that they live in a world of abundance and that they are part of a bigger story, written by a grand giver. Just like the young lion king, the people of our congregation remembered who they were!

When our church treasurer handed out the $500 checks, one by one, under the fluorescent lights of our nondescript fellowship hall, congregants remembered. They remembered when sharing had been part of who they were.

Holding those checks in hand reminded all of us that we belonged to a church that understood its identity. A reader of LaSalle's history could have foreseen those checks coming. The history revealed all the clues: an almost non-existent hierarchy, commitment to on-the-ground and in-the-trenches service, ministries birthed not from the inspired vision of a senior pastor, but from the deep desires and great gifts of individual congregants ready to wear their giver identities on their sleeves. Really, those checks shouldn't have come as a surprise. Sure, the timing presented a surprise. The amount too. But the gift of entrusting its people with every resource it had? LaSalle had operated in the same fashion from day one.

Over lunch that afternoon in Leslie Hall, we as a church

body anticipated together the impact the checks would have on us individually, on our church collectively, and on the causes and programs we would eventually support with the money. We didn't anticipate what was about to occur, though. This was the real surprise—for all of us: LaSallers weren't the only ones remembering generosity's tune.

The Press and the Profound

The week following our Sunday-morning check giveaway, calls began trickling in to the church office. Within two weeks, the phone rang virtually non-stop. Reporters from around the country and around the world wanted to hear the story of a church giving money away. The news of LaSalle's #LoveLetGo campaign, as we had titled the check giveaway,[1] appeared in print on every continent but Antarctica.

Why on earth would people find the story so interesting? Plenty of religious institutions in Chicago, much less across the globe, spend $160,000 on ministries or missions. Plenty of secular organizations invest many times the amount of our giveaway in efforts to improve the collective lot

The news of LaSalle's #LoveLetGo campaign, as we had titled the check giveaway, appeared in print on every continent but Antarctica.

of humankind. By being dispersed across 320 people, our dollars would have *less* of a quantifiable impact than the programs making strides against poverty or human trafficking—though not making headlines.

The novelty of a church giving away money drew some people into the story. But something bigger, something more profound, was evidenced by those ringing phones and full email inboxes. People were beginning to hear generosity's song again. And LoveLetGo had amped up the volume.

When interviewers and reporters asked where the idea originated, our church leaders shared the principle of the tithe, the concept of returning the first 10 percent to the source of the gift. Obedience determined the *amount* given away. But *how* it was given away reflected LaSalle's unique identity as a collection of individuals living out a call, not as an institution led by a few who had been called. Through decades of scarcity, LaSalle's congregation—a motley crew of beggars showing other beggars where to find food—practiced

> Most headlines bring to mind scarcity. In the LoveLetGo headline, generosity trumped scarcity.

generosity. Generosity's imprint marked LaSalle's identity, and the check giveaway was simply another tattoo of generosity on the church's skin.

Most headlines bring to mind scarcity. In the LoveLetGo headline, generosity trumped scarcity. *That* was the real news story, and it was a story of good news. And when people heard the story, they heard not just one church's story. They heard an echo of their own stories. The stories of their youth, when generosity came easily. The stories they caught snippets of in their daily lives, when a stranger held open a door . . . or offered a free hug outside a movie theater.

The reporters weren't telling LaSalle's story. They were telling generosity's story. And the tale felt familiar all over our city, our country, and our world.

Front Doorposts,
Back Entrances

Why does generosity make headlines, catching us by surprise, if it's inscribed in our DNA? If generosity feels familiar, why don't we see more of it? Why don't we hear its tune being hummed by people we pass on the street?

If generosity feels familiar, why don't we see more of it?

Generosity faces formidable competition. You might name several challengers: a culture of consumption, a growing rich-poor gap, the anonymity of social media, increased exposure to advertising. While those factors may impede generosity, they aren't its greatest challenge.

We are.

We battle generosity daily. Not in a fist-fight, actively aggressive way, but subtly, and often without realizing it.

As far back as Abraham and long before the purported villains of social media or a culture of consumption existed, God knew myriad forces would compete for our attention, distracting us from our core identities. The call from Scripture breaks through the busy-ness, the voices, the demands—and the anxiety, fear, and insecurity they often produce. In Deuteronomy 6:5-9, immediately after sharing the Ten Commandments, Moses delivers the Great Commandment to his sisters and brothers:

> We battle generosity daily. Not in a fist-fight, actively aggressive way, but subtly, and often without realizing it.

> You shall love the LORD your God with all your heart, and with all your soul, and with all your might. Keep these words that I am commanding you today in your heart. Recite them to your children and talk about them when you are at home and when you are away, when you lie down and when you rise. Bind them as a sign on your hand, fix them as an emblem on your forehead, and write them on the doorposts of your house and on your gates.

Recite the words! Talk about them! Write them on doorposts! Fix them on your forehead! Then, when you look in the mirror, you will see your true identity reflected. In seeing yourself truly, and fully, you will see the path to generosity. Because it was already there.

But we can't read the words on the front doorpost if we only use the back entrance. We can't see our true identities reflected in the mirror if we don't stop and gaze. We can't hum generosity's tune if another melody is playing in our heads. And even generosity's champions get distracted, like Miriam, Moses's sister.

> *We can't hum generosity's tune if another melody is playing in our heads.*

Miriam, the Bible's first female prophet, possessed all of the characteristics of today's modern woman—clever, confident, independent, born to lead—in a culture valuing none of those traits in women. In her first appearance in Exodus, Miriam employs her wits to save her brother's life and ultimately the lives of the Israelites. Miriam's identity as protector of Moses and her people gets cemented early.

Decades later, Miriam serves as one of the leaders of the Exodus along with Moses and their older brother Aaron. The women in particular follow Miriam. Formerly enslaved in Egypt, these women now march through a barren land, somehow responsible for the care and feeding of the men and children on the journey. They need protection, motivation, and inspiration. You can almost imagine Miriam imploring the women in the desert: *Recite the words! Talk about them! Remem-*

ber my song? The one I sang after we crossed the Red Sea and the waters engulfed our pursuers?

Sing to the LORD, for he has triumphed gloriously; horse and rider he has thrown into the sea. (Exod. 15:21)

Sisters, don't forget! March on and have faith. In staying true to her calling as protector, Miriam remains an anchor of faith for her people under conditions that would challenge the most capable of leaders.

Yet late in the journey, Miriam falters over what seems like a triviality: Moses has taken a non-Israelite as a wife. Giving Miriam the benefit of the doubt, we might assign her response of indignation to patriotism. But the text in Numbers 12:2 suggests otherwise, as Miriam and Aaron ask, "Has the LORD spoken only through Moses? Has he not spoken through us also?" Jealous, Miriam wonders why Moses gets to do as he chooses, even if his choice violates common practice. Her protest stems not from a desire to safeguard the people, but from a desire to protect herself and Aaron. As fellow prophets, they feel their status threatened by Moses's decision. In this small moment, Miriam allows her identity as prophetess to upstage her role as protector.

For decades Miriam was *good*. Better than good. Self-sacrificing and generous, giving everything she had to her people. She got distracted for only a moment! To us, God's response appears harsh: God strikes Miriam with leprosy, forcing the people to cast her out of camp. The march stalls while Miriam is shut out for seven days. For a nomadic people always seeking new sources of food and water, the pause poses risks. The protector has imperiled her people.

But what if the leprosy is a gift of grace, not a punishment? What if God wants Miriam to see her identity anew? To view it from a different perspective. To remember she has lived into her promise for a lifetime—scholars believe Miriam was an octogenarian when cast out of camp—staying true to her mission and people until this moment. Outside the makeshift boundary wall of camp, what might Miriam notice? Perhaps words written on gates and doorposts, words she has recited time and again. The words of generosity's promise to her and to her people.

In her exile from camp, Miriam has time to reflect on her identity without any competing demands for her attention. She can puzzle the pieces of her identity back together, and in doing so, remember that generosity has come easily. She wears its imprint.

Like Miriam, we need reminders. Sometimes those reminders arrive in unexpected forms—like our $500 checks.

Discernment, Fish, and Temptation

The day of the check giveaway, every congregant left Leslie Hall with a $500 check. But how would those checks be spent?

How would the church give away its $1.4 million? Few, perhaps none, of us realized we couldn't answer those questions well without exploring two deeper questions: Who am I? and Who is LaSalle? Although no one would call LaSallers a shallow bunch, neither would anyone consider LaSalle's culture to foster navel-gazing. We don't spend a lot of time wringing our hands over doctrine or arguing eschatological views. Our debates tend to be about the best course of action, not about whether to act. For a church used to jumping in with both feet, pondering our identity might have seemed to some like a waste of time.

But it was something we needed to do in order to give away our money with open eyes as well as open hearts. So the table adjacent to the treasurer's table was piled high with copies of Elizabeth Liebert's *The Way of Discernment*. Many of us opened the book excited to see a list of practices. Awesome—a to-do list! As if she wrote the book with action-oriented people like us in mind.

Not so fast.

Following the list is a simple but hard-to-follow command: Stop. Remember who you are. "Great desires, passions, motivations, loves and hates, and the decisions that flow from them—this is the stuff of discernment!" Liebert says.[2] Sure, decision-making includes practices—actions—but those pieces become fruitful only *after* understanding our identity. If in our decision-making process we wanted to experience authentic generosity, the kind of generosity that sparks joy for the giver and the recipient, we needed to know ourselves first.

The book would help congregants know themselves better, but the church, too, needed to reconnect with its collective identity. With $500 checks and discernment books in hand, congregants approached seventeen poster-sized, ocean-themed papers covering two walls in Leslie Hall. Each sheet depicted a type of fish and bore the name of the leader of a prayer group—a "school of fish." Congregants signed up to be part of a school, and with each school consisting of no more than twenty people, the groups offered a venue for shared discernment, bridging the gap between private, individual reflection and whole-church decision-making.

If in our decision-making process we wanted to experience authentic generosity, the kind of generosity that sparks joy for the giver and the recipient, we needed to know ourselves first.

Then, over the following months, we worked through the discernment book individually and together, trying on for size the various suggested practices. In the fish schools we began talking about and reflecting on our identities. We pondered our desires and passions and loves and hates. We saw ourselves reflected in the mirrors of our fellow congregants around the table. And we started to ask who we were and who LaSalle was.

In the process, people rediscovered or reinforced the identity threads clearly connecting the events of their lives, including Jane Lambshead. Jane's early experiences growing up outside a largely segregated Washington D.C. gave her a love and concern for those who lacked basic resources, individuals who were marginalized—and that thread never frayed in her. A second-grade teacher most of her adult life, upon retirement Jane spent a year teaching orphans in a remote fishing village in Kenya. Helping these underdog kids drew on her teaching experience and fed a long-standing interest in anthropology she had left unexplored since college.

In the few weeks prior to receiving her $500 check, Jane had learned of a ministry in northern Africa—where Christians represent a small minority—focused on training local Christians to share the gospel. Her $500 gift bought Bibles for the new believers. Jane used her check to connect long-knit threads in her life: her heart for disenfranchised people, a curiosity about other cultures, and her belief in the power of a one-on-one transformative teaching relationship.

You may wonder how David Melia used his five hundred dollars. You might guess he supported his hugging ministry with the funds, perhaps by taking another tour. He didn't. He extended beyond hugs. As a person who understands his identity, David spent his first hundred dollars taking people out for coffee, getting to know them, hearing about their passions, and finding ways he could encourage their efforts. His belief in the power of random acts of kindness tied hugs and coffees together.

Some LaSallers knew themselves well enough to jump in like Jane and David did with their five hundred dollars. Many more of us needed time and space, though, to consider who we were as people and as givers. Multiply $500 by 320 people, and you can imagine the challenge we faced as a church with the $1.4 million windfall.

Like Miriam, we found staying true to ourselves can prove difficult. Looking back at LaSalle in the last months of 2014, we saw our little church making headlines, including the front page of the *Chicago Tribune* on Christmas morning. We wrestled with the temptation to see our church differently—"Wow, we really are something! Maybe we've launched a movement!" We easily could have added spin to the story so LaSalle became the star of the show. We easily could have forgotten the core identity prompting the reverse tithe in the first place.

When we believed ourselves to be at the center of the story, we felt tempted to make big plans, "needing" to uphold our newfound reputation as a church making radical news. More than once, we had to ask ourselves: Are we considering this idea because it will satisfy the public's interest in our story, or because this is God's call for our church? Are we simply stroking our collective ego? For

Like Miriam, we found staying true to ourselves can prove difficult.

people who take their faith walk seriously, these are sobering questions. We didn't want to become generosity's most formidable obstacle.

As our church wrestled with the question of how we would spend the remaining windfall, we intentionally rooted ourselves in identity. We listened closely for ideas aligned with an element of LaSalle's DNA, the characteristics we talked over in our fish schools: sharing the gospel, meeting immediate needs, advocating for others and for Jesus, addressing racial and economic disparity, and reducing violence. All of the elements had been tied together by strings of generosity. Our attempt to root ourselves reflected our desire to stay true to our core identity as a church. Whether or not the press found it newsworthy.

As our church wrestled with the question of how we would spend the remaining windfall, we intentionally rooted ourselves in identity.

For most of us, remembering who we are won't be prompted by surprise $500 checks, nor will we make headline news in the process. But we will feel the elation of surprise and the satisfaction of recognition. Even more so, we will feel grateful, and we'll start looking for recipients of our gratitude because generosity's tune will be playing in our heads.

CHAPTER 5

TRANSACTIONS AND INTERACTIONS

Pick an average day of the past week and think about how many people you interacted with that day. Count everyone, even if your encounter lasted only briefly, perhaps just the time it took you to buy a cup of coffee or check out at the grocery store. Depending on your activities, you may encounter dozens, if not hundreds, of people. Bosses, employees, colleagues. Cashiers, customers, managers. Students, teachers, administrators. Bus drivers, police officers, garbage collectors. Outside our homes especially, we tend to view people through the identities they wear relative to us. We expect certain behaviors of people wearing certain labels. On a daily basis we honor unspoken boundaries, guidelines, and rules of engagement.

When we recognize our own identities as givers, we start seeing others differently.

Yet when we recognize our own identities as givers, we start seeing others differently. Our framework of interpretation shifts, and we expand beyond the confines of labels and ground rules. We begin to see the roles other people play in the same story of generosity in which we participate. The re-framing becomes contagious—others also begin to see us, themselves, and the world differently, as LaSallers discovered in giving away their five hundred dollars.

Dan West plays many roles at LaSalle, but most of our congregants know him as the Voice of God. Often when a Scripture passage calls for God's voice, we enlist Dan, whose robust and resonant timbre keeps us at rapt attention. Dan also epitomizes the model image of the gentle grandfather, with his warm smile, hearty laugh, and billowy, milky-white beard.

After weeks of reflecting on how to use his LoveLetGo check, Dan felt compelled to start giving away his money in person, twenty dollars at a time, with his own hands. Rather than donating to a non-profit organization to do great work, which certainly would have honored the intent of the campaign, Dan wanted to do the work directly himself.

On his first trek into his local neighborhood, after meandering the streets for two hours with twenty dollars still nestled in his pocket, Dan came across a daycare center bearing this sign: *Naptime 1–2:30. Please do not ring the bell. Knock quietly.*

The middle-aged woman who opened the door upon Dan's gentle tapping had a spit-up stain on her shoulder, and her weary countenance suggested she needed a nap as much as the children. Dan explained why he had come, saying, "I thought maybe you would know of someone among the parents of these children who really needs it."

"Nah. I don't know nobody like that," she responded as she began to close the door. Determined, Dan held out the twenty dollars, insisting he didn't want anything in return, he wasn't selling something, he just wanted the money to do some good.

What makes us suspicious of a grandfatherly figure who comes to the door offering money? Why does our fear radar activate, setting off warnings to be vigilant in the face of danger? When someone comes to the door offering twenty dollars, we presume he or she expects twenty dollars' worth of something in return.

Except Dan didn't expect a thing. He was peddling grace.

Getting Close Enough to See

Like Dan, other LaSallers extended themselves in the process of giving away their five hundred dollars. The majority of our congregants chose to spend their money on an individual or a cause they felt personally connected to and wanted to engage with more intentionally. They sought to *deepen relationships* in the process of giving away money.

The longing for connection and relationship contrasts with our typical transactions—much of the time we *actively avoid* establishing connection. Thanks to the self-serve checkout at the grocery store, the ATMs or phones we utilize as bank tellers, and the ability to purchase almost everything online, we no longer need to know the person who sits on the other end of a transaction. Within our homes and offices, we find ourselves communicating via text or email with someone sitting several feet away. Given the ease with which we can avoid interactions, we might wonder if any attempt to live relationally is fighting a losing battle.

But in the generous life, proximity and relationship matter.

Photographer Christopher Jacobs got close to a group of men many people might fear or disdain: twelve prisoners at the Cook County Jail in Chicago.[1] He had received an assignment to photograph the newly installed executive director of the department, Dr. Nneka Jones Tapia. Her appointment was notable not only because she was female and African-American, but also because she is believed to be the first clinical psychologist to run a major jail or prison—and Cook County boasts the largest jail in the country.

Given the ease with which we can avoid interactions, we might wonder if any attempt to live relationally is fighting a losing battle. But in the generous life, proximity and relationship matter.

Jacobs's interaction with Dr. Jones Tapia left him floored. At the end of their conversation, deeply impressed by her ideas and her vision, he asked if he could volunteer at the jail. A few months later, Jacobs became a teacher, helping twelve inmates see the world from behind a camera lens. Twice a month, he spent two hours at the prison with his students. The class culminated in an exhibit, held in the jail's gymnasium, unemotionally titled "1st Cook County Jail Mental Health Transition Center Photography Exhibit."

But emotions ran high in that room.

Not only were the walls covered with photos taken by the students; they also bore photos *of* the students—not in their prison garb, but in sport coats that Jacobs had bought for them. Jacobs, who has captured images of icons like Eric Clapton and Buddy Guy, took each prisoner's photo with the same attention and care.

Jacobs's story was featured in the *Chicago Tribune* on Valentine's Day 2016. And it was truly a love story.

"Will it change their lives? I don't know," Jacobs said. "But this experience has changed my life. I have taken photos of very cool people, been in a lot of cool places. But this is the coolest thing I have ever done, and I am going to keep doing it."[2]

Jacobs saw these men differently. He didn't see criminals or thieves or drug dealers. He saw artists. Because he was close enough to see.

Getting close takes effort. More effort than we likely even realize. You may be familiar with the term "priming." Social scientists apply this term to the subconscious or non-conscious influences that affect our behavior. Here's a quick example—the

STUMBLING TOWARD GENEROSITY

word "soup." Because you just read that word in this book, if
someone later today asked you what five items a household typ-
ically stocks in its pantry, you
would be more likely to in-
clude "soup" in your response
than if you had not seen the
word recently. As you might
guess, the priming effect proves tremendously difficult to over-
come. Psychologist Kathleen Vohs and her colleagues wanted
to understand the subconscious influence of money, given its
ubiquitous presence in our lives.

Getting close takes effort.
More effort than we likely
even realize.

Vohs and her team conducted nine experiments during
which they primed some participants with the idea of money.[3]
In one experiment, participants sat down in front of computers to fill out questionnaires. After six minutes, a screensaver
appeared on some of the computers. Some participants saw
images of money floating underwater, some saw fish swimming underwater, and others saw no screensaver at all. After
the participants completed the questionnaires, each of them
next set up two chairs: one for him or herself, and another for a
second participant who would soon enter for a get-acquainted
conversation.

Would you like to venture a guess about the distance between the chairs, depending on the screensaver image some
participants saw? Those primed with the brief, subconscious
image of money placed their chairs more than one foot farther

apart, almost 50 percent farther apart than unprimed participants. The take-away: Exposure to the mere image of money distances us physically from others, without our conscious awareness.

If money distances us physically, what does it do to us emotionally? And how can we possibly see others' true identities if we fail to lean in close?

Hoping we possess more power over our actions than a screensaver does, you may insist, *Well, that's just one experiment!* But all nine experiments by Vohs and her colleagues demonstrated similar results, with money-primed participants acting more independently than unprimed subjects. From picking up pencils an experimenter dropped, to helping explain directions to someone, to choosing between leisure activities designed for one person versus multiple people, money-primed people behaved in ways confirming their self-sufficiency.[4]

If money distances us physically, what does it do to us emotionally? And how can we possibly see others' true identities if we fail to lean in close?

While we want to believe better of ourselves, we recognize the reality of our day-to-day lives. Many in-person, face-to-face interactions involve money—as a topic of conversation over the dinner table, as the form of exchange in a transaction, or as the backdrop of a decision we make with a co-worker. Often, for one reason or another, we have money on our minds before an interaction even begins. As intentionally as we may choose to live, most of us find money's presence unavoidable.

No wonder that childcare worker nearly closed the door on Dan. Her involuntary, subconscious mind-set prevented her from seeing Dan for who he was—one beggar showing another where to find food.

Keeping Score

Dan's encounter affirms how the mention of money increases our likelihood to want to keep our distance from others. But it also demonstrates an insidious assumption we make in the presence of money: someone wins and someone loses—also known as a zero-sum game. At the gas station, we expect the twenty dollars departing our wallet to line the station's cash register at the close of the transaction. The twenty dollars won't suddenly transform into twenty-five dollars, nor will it unexpectedly drop to fifteen dollars. (Even if an unscrupulous cashier palms five bucks, the total sum of money gained equals the twenty dollars lost by the customer. The positive "gained" twenty dollars plus the negative "lost" twenty dollars equals zero—hence the term "zero sum.")

With zero-sum games, keeping score seems pretty straight-forward. If we work for a company offering year-end bonuses, we know that if our colleague down the hall gets more, then we get less. High school seniors applying to college recognize that if a classmate wins a spot, they're more likely to be on the losing end of the admissions lottery. Even young children breaking open a piñata at a birthday party realize that every piece of candy snatched by another preschooler means one fewer treat for them.

Part of us *likes* keeping score. We like to know where we stand. We like the concrete, definitive nature of wins and losses. We like setting targets for ourselves and for our lives. At the heart of it, we like keeping score because we believe scores tell a story. And in a zero-sum world, the story features winners and losers. Haves and have-nots. Us and them.

And the story is centuries old.

Keeping score, after all, is an ancient sport among the human race. Consider King David of the Old Testament, fondly called "a man after God's own heart." When we first meet David, he tends the family's flock of sheep in the fields. Despite his unexceptional beginnings, David catapults onto the scene as the victor over Goliath, the conqueror of invading armies, and, ultimately, the king of a united Israel. In the world of zero-sum games, he merits the title "winner."

> At the heart of it, we like keeping score because we believe scores tell a story. And in a zero-sum world, the story features winners and losers.

Given his meteoric rise, David deserves to feel proud of how far he and his nation have come under his leadership.

Yet in psalm after psalm, David sings God's praises. He thanks God repeatedly and unabashedly for the graces and gifts he has received. David's consistent message in every breath: *Not by my hand but by yours,* LORD, have these blessings come.

Until the day David begins to wonder. In 2 Samuel 24, David tells his commander Joab to take a census of the people "so that I may know how many there are." David has a hunch he can tell an epic story with the numbers. By keeping score, he can document the story he believes the figures will tell: *Your kingdom, David, is huge. Massive. Well done.* After the counting is complete, a mere ten verses later, David awakens to his hubris. "Stricken to the heart," he pleads with God for forgiveness, acknowledging, *I let the story become about me.*

Keeping score separates us from each other, from God, and from our core identities as givers. It moves our proverbial chairs farther apart.

But even without money, or winning or losing on our minds, we may still avoid getting close to others because, let's face it, getting along can be *hard*. Coming together can mean disagreement and tension and mistrust. Church communities—LaSalle included—are as susceptible to conflict as any other community, especially when the conflicts revolve around money. At the same time, something powerful can happen in community. Something mysterious, magical, and unique. People wearing their giver identities see each other and the bigger story clearly, and generosity gets a chance to work unchecked, as LaSalle evidenced in 2002, more than a decade before the million-dollar windfall.

At that time, Atrium Village was one of several real-estate projects of the church. The only one we walked in and out of on a regular basis as a congregation was our community center building, which housed our church offices and the offices of many local ministries. With no windfall in sight on any investment, we stood knee-deep in debt on the community center, and our largest tenants—our own ministries—had continually failed to make rent payments. Refinancing the mortgage represented the sole lifeboat on our sinking ship, but a church with a history of being broke doesn't inspire banks to cut a deal.

In walked an offer from a major Christian institution. The proposal would provide us much-needed cash in exchange for the sale of our community center, including a twenty-five-year lease gradually reducing our footprint in the building. We confronted a decision none of us wanted to make. Our choice not only would impact us acutely but also would determine LaSalle's future.

The night before the deadline for a decision, our two governing boards convened together. Every board member had studied the facts; we had met frequently for weeks; the boards understood the nuances of the offer and its implications. Yet this well-versed, well-informed group of twenty-some church members couldn't agree.

For hours we debated how to proceed. We heard arguments of logic and arguments of passion. We talked about missions and mortgages. We laughed and cried and prayed.

As midnight approached, we had to take a vote. The motion was made to accept the deal. "All in favor?" asked the moderator of our deacon board. Some of the smartest, wisest people in the room raised their hands. "All opposed?" And again, some of the smartest, wisest people there raised their hands.

The motion failed to pass. By one vote.

We had saved our building. But what had we done to nearly half our leaders who had advocated to accept the deal? These beloved fellow church members who had devoted hour upon hour to educating us on the facts and to negotiating on our behalf—had we just made them losers? Did they feel like they had come up empty after a zero-sum transaction?

One of the most profound lessons we have learned about generosity happened in the ninety seconds following that vote. The two people who had been the leading advocates for accepting the deal turned to each other and to their fellow board members and asked, "How is 7:30 tomorrow morning for a call to get plan B rolling?"

No cursing under the breath or nursing a wound or simmering in the mire of defeat. To them, the vote represented not a zero-sum game of winners and losers, but an exercise of discernment among good-hearted, God-loving, faith-seeking human beings they considered their spiritual brothers and sisters. They wore their God-given identities at the table. Despite their day jobs in the market and their facility with its ground rules, they opted to see their interactions as an opportunity for relationships to trump transactions. They had no interest in keeping score. They knew what counted in the moment, and they honored it.

Proximity, Apart

Today's technology facilitates connection. Our devices keep us within reach any time of day or night. We contact friends and family on opposite sides of the globe with a few taps on a keyboard. Our gadgets hold the power to bring us closer, but they also keep us apart.

In his book *Are You Fully Charged?* best-selling author Tom Rath notes that people check their cell phones an average of 110 times a day.[5] In addition to wreaking havoc on our ability to work efficiently, this habit hinders our focus on the people we interact with every day. Research shows that the mere presence of a cell phone reduces the amount of dialogue during and satisfaction with an in-person conversation. As often as we use social media to facilitate meaningful connection, we've likely seen it employed as a popularity contest of "likes" and "connections" and "followers."

LaSaller Eric Larson chose to intentionally extend and create connection—via a device. In October 2014, one month after our LoveLetGo giveaway, a missionary he friended on Facebook posted a plea for a woman named Fatou. Abandoned by her husband and family because of a leg injury rendering her incapable of typical women's work, Fatou traveled the country, trying various indigenous healing methods to no avail. At the end of her thirteen-year exodus, she ended up in the town where Eric's contact, Linnea, served.

Linnea depleted her benevolence fund to support Fatou's treatment, which involved heavy antibiotics and daily redressing of her ulcerous leg. After treatment, the doctors determined amputation presented the sole option to save Fatou's life. When Linnea posted Fatou's story, she asked for donations of any amount toward the cost of the surgery. That's when Eric reached out, asking how much in total was needed for the operation. The response: five hundred dollars.

The figure got Eric's attention. And Fatou received her amputation.

In November, Fatou recovered from surgery. She spent much of her time with her new friends in Linnea's community, sharing her story of grace. After thirteen years of exile, Fatou lived fully and happily.

But in the last two weeks of December, Fatou's health took

a devastating turn, and in early January she fell into a coma. On January 12 she died, most probably from metastatic cancer.

When he heard the news, Eric wrote, "I felt like I failed because the funds didn't buy a cure." Because Eric works at a rehab hospital, he knew how long the recovery would take, he envisioned what the rehab process would be like, he estimated when Fatou would be healthy enough for a prosthetic leg, and he imagined a future for her, including worthy work and perhaps a new or reunited family.

In his moment of feeling like a failure, Eric's transactional framework prevailed. This was far from a storybook

Even when living generously, we are tempted to keep score.

ending: Fatou had lost her life, and he had lost a nobly desired outcome for her. Also, as Eric freely admitted, he felt like he had lost face, because other LaSallers would be coming back to church sharing incredible stories of impact from their $500 gifts. Even when living generously, we are tempted to keep score.

Yet generosity has a bigger story. What looks like failure to us is recast. After some reflection, Eric saw tremendous victory in the final chapter. Fatou might have died alone and desperate; instead, she passed in a community of people whom she loved and

Our transactional, zero-sum rules fall short when measuring what really counts.

who loved her back. Our transactional, zero-sum rules fall short when measuring what really counts.

Eric never traveled to Africa. He never met Linnea. He never had the opportunity to meet Fatou. Yet through giving, he had a fledgling connection he wanted to nurture. Generosity brought what was far, close. What was apart, within proximity.

After Dan West pleaded with the woman at the childcare center, she kept the door open. She listened to Dan, leaning in as he repeated his purpose. He only wanted to give the money to someone who could use it, and surely she knew a family in need. She hesitated. She paused. Silence filled the seconds.

Finally she asked, "Could I keep it and use it myself?"

It wasn't the response Dan expected. "Well, are you really the person here who needs it the most?" he asked.

"Yes. I believe I am," she replied.

So Dan leaned in, too, and put the twenty dollars into her hands. She blessed him and called him an angel, saying she never thought she would see an angel. With tears in his eyes, Dan blessed her back and walked home with an empty pocket.

The twenty dollars Dan handed the childcare worker cost Dan far less than twenty dollars and rewarded the woman far more than twenty dollars. When two givers interact, the ground rules change. A transaction becomes more than a simple exchange; the value gets amplified.

We may be primed to keep score, but when we choose to keep close, our perspective alters, offering us a view into our fellow givers' stories that stretches past their surface labels. That's what LaSallers began to see when they gave of themselves along with their checks. They caught a vision of something else, too: they had more to give.

We may be primed to keep score, but when we choose to keep close, our perspective alters, offering us a view into our fellow givers' stories that stretches past their surface labels.

CHAPTER 6

THE SATURATION POINT

Defying the doctrine of scarcity, LaSalle's peddlers of grace kept restocking the shelves. Dozens of LaSallers supplemented or matched their $500 checks either by using their own funds or by recruiting friends and family to contribute. Even more congregants volunteered their time and energy to the recipient of their gift.

Generosity caused them to believe they had more to give. Giving made them feel full. Sounds illogical, doesn't it? But by receiving and then turning over the five hundred dollars, these congregants reframed *all* of their resources. The dollars they gave through LoveLetGo looked awfully similar to the dollars sitting in their wallets and bank accounts. Why couldn't they give away those other dollars, too? In viewing every cent as a grace gift, this group of LaSallers made a discovery: they had enough. They had reached their saturation point and could share the rest.

The saturation point feels especially elusive in Western society. We find ourselves prodded to investigate the benefits of *more*: ads explicitly aimed at our wallets; movies and television shows linking products to characters' happiness; and the infamous Joneses who "shared" their latest acquisition on social media. In a world characterized by rapid technological improvement in goods like phones, homes, and cars, as well as in advances like renewable energy and genetic testing, how could we possibly stop wanting more, when more means better quality of life not just for ourselves but potentially for all humankind?

> The saturation point feels especially elusive in Western society. We find ourselves prodded to investigate the benefits of **more**.

While you or people you know may skillfully resist the messages of more, collectively we've had a rough time reaching the saturation point. Home sizes have increased, self-storage rental units have proliferated to accommodate our stuff, and consumer debt has outpaced income by 15 percent.[1] People at LaSalle Street Church are no exception. More than a handful of our churchgoers have found themselves in financial counseling followed by overhauls to their budgets. Being Christian doesn't inoculate us from the messages of consumption. Scarcity's sweater commands attention, regardless of who wears it.

But wait, you might respond, *I'm not interested in more stuff. Having more money means I could save for retirement or for my kids' educations, or give more to charity. I'd finally feel financially secure.*

Many of us believe our saturation point resides on the other side of the next pay raise, or the next bonus, or the next job. But our beliefs are belied by research, as even the uber-rich say they need more cash to reach the nirvana of financial security: people with $1 million in net worth seek $2 million; those at $10 million aspire for $25 million.[2] Eighty-four percent of millionaires believe themselves to belong to the middle class or upper middle class, not the upper class.[3] As incomes rise, perspectives shift. What once felt extravagant becomes an expectation. What once seemed luxurious becomes standard.[4] Regardless of our good intentions about giving more or working less when we reach a target income level, turning a deaf ear to the sounds of scarcity proves tougher than we expect. Meanwhile, in the background, generosity lingers, humming its familiar tune.

Being Christian doesn't inoculate us from the messages of consumption.

Memories and Masters

One of the Bible's early lessons on enough comes from the story of the Exodus. As the Israelites flee Egypt en route to the Promised Land, they find food and water scarce. They question Moses: *Did you lead us out of slavery so that we could starve to death instead?* In response, God assures Moses of his presence and provision. Every day, when the sun rises, the ground will be blanketed with food. The catch? Each person is to take only what is needed for the day. *Trust me*, God says, *you will all have enough*. The manna will suffice. You will have the means to march on, to care for your families, to feel full.

For several generations, the Israelites in Egypt faced scarcity at every turn, as if in a funhouse hall of mirrors with every visible surface reflecting scarcity's sweater. *But we've never had enough,* some surely thought. *Wouldn't prudence dictate we save a share of bread for the morning?*

> Trust me, God says, you will all have enough.

God freed the Israelites from slavery in Egypt. Yet in the wilderness, they proceeded to enslave themselves. Disregarding Moses's instructions, some stashed away part of the manna until morning, and "it bred worms and became foul" (Exod. 16:20). When they took more than they needed or stored it away for safe-keeping, they placed their faith in the manna, not in the God who liberated them from slavery, or in the ground producing their breakfast each morning. In a world of scarcity, resourcefulness counts. Can you feel God's heart ache as the people hoard the manna and judge the saturation point to be just out of reach?

Some of us live paycheck to paycheck, dreading the next unexpected expense from a car repair or an appliance break-down. Others of us watch the see-saw of our investment savings with angst, wondering if retirement is a dream unlikely to come true. Fear has an ongoing grip. It held the Israelites and holds many of us, especially around the topic of money. And because a church is simply a collection of individuals, fearful people make fearful churches.

At LaSalle, a committee of eleven people comprised a leadership council tasked with recommending a plan for our big windfall to our governing board and, ultimately, to our congregation. Every month of our discernment process, the leadership council reviewed a report from the "fish schools" that included the groups' reflections on Scripture readings, thoughts on LaSalle's role in the neighborhood, feedback on the process, and ideas for distributing the money. As members of the leadership council, we reviewed the reports in advance of our meetings and would spend our in-person time together talking over elements we found particularly intriguing or insightful.

In the first few reports, our council identified a handful of themes, one of which was sustainability. People wanted whatever we would pursue as a congregation to last beyond the current staff and members. The money's impact should reach past our walls and our time, much like the original Atrium Village investment did. As the congregation began to talk about sustainability, one idea came up frequently: pay off the mortgage on our community center building. Eliminating our mortgage debt would virtually guarantee future cash flow for the church, and as we entered December with a budget shortfall of fifty thousand dollars, this idea looked increasingly appealing.

As a leadership council, we heartily endorsed the value of sustainability. While we weren't opposed to taking risks with the funds in the form of supporting new ministries, we agreed with the congregation's desire to foster deep and lasting change as a result of the way we apportioned the money. Given the goal of sustainability, the idea of paying off the mortgage made logical sense. But something didn't feel right, and it took us several meetings and much praying to figure out why we kept getting stuck in our discussions.

In his Sermon on the Mount, Jesus covers a myriad of topics—divorce, prayer, fasting, giving, and the Golden Rule, among others. While the term "saturation point" isn't named in the sermon, Jesus addresses the idea:

No one can serve two masters; for a slave will either hate the one and love the other, or be devoted to the one and despise the other. You cannot serve God and wealth. Therefore I tell you, do not worry about your life, what you will eat or what you will drink, or about your body, what you will wear. Is not life more than food, and the body more than clothing? Look at the birds of the air; they neither sow nor reap nor gather into barns, and yet your Father feeds them. Are you not of more value than they? And can any of you by worrying add a single hour to your span of life? . . . So do not worry about tomorrow, for tomorrow will bring worries of its own. Today's trouble is enough for today. (Matt. 6:24-27, 34)

We reach the saturation point when we stop worrying about tomorrow.

We reach the saturation point when we let go of fear of want.

We reach the saturation point when we recall what we have.

We reach the saturation point when we serve God today, addressing today's troubles, and leave tomorrow's for tomorrow.

As we debated paying off the mortgage, we had to face the question of why we wanted to eliminate the debt. Was our primary motivation to enable the church to tackle transformative projects and take bold risks in the future, or was the real objective to reduce our fears and anxieties today?

We reach the saturation point when we let go of fear of want.

We had just received an enormous windfall. More money than the church could ever have imagined. And here we sat, afraid. Afraid of how we'd make budget by the end of the year. Afraid of what we would have to give up if we didn't. Afraid of tomorrow's trouble. The immediate fear made our collective memory short. We saw scarcity ahead and forgot the abundance right behind us.

Paying off debt might have made sense for a different church, but for LaSalle, paying off debt would have been a nod to the wrong master. Rather than trusting in God, we would have demonstrated trust in our bank account. Rather than seeing the bigger backdrop, we would have been looking dead-on at scarcity in the mirror. The windfall, we became convinced, needed to address today's troubles and not become tomorrow's security blanket.

But we also needed to be responsible stewards and not become the proverbial cobbler whose children go shoeless. So our church set aside $100,000 of the remaining funds to allow our property and finance committee to assess our future financial needs, with the goal to build and perhaps seed-fund a sustainable plan to meet those needs. In this decision, fear wasn't our master. Or security. We recognized we had ignored today's troubles for years, allowing our buildings to age without thoughtful maintenance or a plan for improvements. The $100,000 would allow us to catch up with yesterday's troubles. Tomorrow's troubles we trusted we could handle when the time came.

The Contented Life

Generosity doesn't preclude prudence or planning. Conducting a three-year traveling ministry on a shoestring budget certainly required some advance planning by Jesus and his disciples. Nor does generosity preclude the occasional indulgence. Think about the beauty around us, the unnecessary extravagance we experience in the form of lush evergreens and fragrant blossoms and glistening sunlight and melodic birdsong. Indulgences abound on earth. Both planning and indulgence can live alongside generosity, as long as we mark our saturation point.

But that's knowing the unknowable, you might understandably protest. *How can I determine the point when I have enough until I get there? And what if my circumstances change dramatically between now and then? What if I fail to predict how my needs might shift—say, because of an illness or unexpected event?* None of us can see into the future. But we can see today's blessings.

Recall that studies show most of us, even people with multi-million-dollar incomes, want more money to feel content. Today's blessings don't quite cut it, and apparently tomorrow's won't either, because if tomorrow we receive more, we will desire more. Which explains the finding

> Both planning and indulgence can live alongside generosity, as long as we mark our saturation point.

that above $50,000 in earnings, people report the same level of emotional well-being no matter how much they earn.[5] Once we have the resources to meet our basic needs and perhaps indulge a few wants, our contentment level stays remarkably fixed no matter how much money flows into our accounts. If our day-to-day happiness remains the same whether we make $50,000 or $500,000, what saturation point makes sense?

STUMBLING TOWARD GENEROSITY

Perhaps exactly the point where we find ourselves at this moment.

If today's troubles are enough for today, are today's blessings enough, too? Many LaSallers answered yes. In a fresh and novel way, the $500 checks reminded them of the source of every blessing. The surprise windfall awakened congregants, re-opening their eyes to the amazement of each new morning, the beauty of each conversation, and the wonder of having their needs met day in and day out. They had enough, and in the epiphany of saturation, they felt called to respond. With generosity.

If everyone making $50,000 a year felt saturated, imagine how much generosity would be unleashed in the world. If every surprise windfall or increase in take-home pay promptly left the bank account to be repurposed as a gift to someone in need, imagine what local and global problems might be solved!

Instead of waiting for contentment to arrive with the next job or raise or bonus, we can *choose* contentment. As the apostle Paul said in his letter to the Philippians, "I have learned to be content with whatever I have. I know what it is to have little, and I know what it is to have plenty. In any and all circumstances I have learned the secret of being well-fed and of going hungry, of having plenty and of being in need" (Phil. 4:11-12). Unlike the moving target of financial security, contentment offers stability—a sturdy branch we can grip to escape the quicksand of wanting more.

Of course, not everyone's financial settings offer the branch of contentment. Those living at or near minimum wage often face challenging decisions with their checkbooks. People supporting elderly parents or dealing with unemployment or managing a health crisis often experience tremendous economic strain. In the United States, poverty's tentacles grip women and children disproportionately, preventing them from reaching a saturation point. For many people, financial contentment truly may be on the other side of the next job or pay raise. And generosity for these individuals and families may look like freely accepting gifts from others who have plenty to share.

But for others, arresting the feelings of scarcity comes only by giving. When we feel cash poor, we sense we're richer by giving money away. When we feel short on time, we perceive ourselves freer when we volunteer our hours. When we feel sapped of emotional energy, we become refueled by attending closely to another person's life. The psychological research supports this truth, but likely you've experienced this in your life already. Generosity resets the saturation point and offers contentment—in plenty and in need. And at LaSalle, we saw both with the $500 check giveaway.

Generosity resets the saturation point and offers contentment—in plenty and in need.

Filled to Capacity

Every person actively involved in our church received a $500 check, including Stephen Martin. Stephen frequents our midweek meal for the homeless, having spent nearly a decade living under a viaduct in one of Chicago's largest parks before finding transitional shelter in a local YMCA. Though Stephen is resource-poor, he is time-rich, and he spends many of his hours creating art—long-form comics in the espionage genre—a talent inspired by and honed on the streets. While Stephen often holds a pen in his hand, he seldom carries a $500 check bearing his name on the payee line.

Though we instructed congregants to go do God's work with their checks, we also recognized some of God's work might need to be done among our own people. If a member or someone in their family faced a particular hardship, they might very well be called to spend the money on themselves. And as a church, we trusted the discernment process and our congregants. If Stephen had spent time in discernment and decided to use the money toward meeting his basic needs like food, clothing, and medicine, our community would have happily affirmed his decision. We even would have supported him had he chosen to purchase art supplies for his books, knowing the validation he received through his art.

He chose neither. When Stephen received his $500 check, he knew exactly what to do with it. He headed back to the viaduct and rounded up his buddies. "We went out to the show and then to a real restaurant meal. Whatever they wanted to do. For the whole day it didn't feel like they were homeless. All I needed was the hotel! We couldn't afford that. But it was a good feeling to help somebody out like that," Stephen shared. "I remembered what it felt like when people would give me something—money or food. So when I got my check, I turned around and helped a bunch of friends of mine."

Stephen understood the power of validation better than we did. He knew how inconsequential and invisible a homeless person might feel on any given day. *With his five hundred dollars, he made his friends feel like themselves.* Taking them to places where they would be served, where their presence would be acknowledged, where they would be treated like anyone else walking in the door. Where they might remember that they, too, play a role in a bigger narrative.

If we dressed in Stephen's beat-up, worn-out shoes, how many of us would have made the same choice with the money? Most of us look at Stephen's life and see want. See need. See someone barely keeping his head above water. But Stephen saw it differently. He had enough. He was saturated. And because he felt full, his $500 check could overflow to others.

Over the past two decades, we've seen a number of saturation points manifest in the lives of fellow congregants at LaSalle. Lives perhaps a lot like yours. Young adults in their twenties, saddled with student loans, exercise the discipline to save rather than live a lifestyle out of their reach. Married couples opt for one parent to stay home to raise their children, sacrificing many of the perks of having two incomes. People sell their cars or hold onto them well over a decade, when they easily could afford to retain or replace their vehicles. Young professionals who could live in elegant single apartments choose instead to live in modest dwellings with roommates. And seniors find a way to place an offering in the plate each week despite living on a fixed income.

Some LaSallers discovered their saturation points only by necessity. Despite their best intentions, they gradually slipped deeper and deeper into credit card debt. In some cases, a surprise home repair was needed or an illness kept them out of work; in others, they simply desired a little bit more—a new computer, a piece of furniture that wasn't a hand-me-down, a few more meals out.

In 2013, Kristen Metz knew she was in over her head when she and her husband could no longer pay the minimum amount on their credit cards. "I was starting to get phone calls from debt collectors," she recalled. "I was on a slope that I was unable to crawl back up on my own." They were casualties of the housing market crash in 2008, owning a home they couldn't sell. Then the job that helped support the home disappeared, and they moved across the country for new employment. Paying a mortgage of nearly $1,000 a month for the unoccupied home, on top of the rent for their new dwelling, meant that Kristen used credit cards for basic expenses like food and utilities.

In this tenuous financial position, Kristen felt like "we were our own charity." She can recount times when people anonymously dropped off groceries or slipped envelopes with cash under the door.

Yet she and her husband gave. "It felt like miniscule amounts, but it was important that we still had that discipline," Kristen said. Because they had limited financial resources, they gave more generously of their time and their space—coaching local sports teams and inviting college students who couldn't return home during winter break to live with them rent-free.

When the phone calls from debt collectors started coming, Kristen enlisted the help of a credit counseling organization. They developed a plan that she and her husband had been following for over a year when together they received $1,000 in LoveLetGo checks. The easy decision would have been for them to make a major debt payment, allowing them some breathing room. No one would have blinked if they had opted to use some of the money for an indulgence—something they hadn't been able to fund on their own for years. But they gave the money away—to a friend's pet rescue organization.

"We could have used that thousand dollars. But there's that amazing feeling of giving something big. We hadn't been able to do that together ever in our marriage," added Kristen.

"I didn't want to give to my own charity fund. I wanted to be investing in someone else."

In January 2016, Kristen received a letter from the credit counselor beginning with these words: "Congratulations! You have accomplished something you should be proud of." She and her husband had, after six austere years, paid off their debt and could start fresh. And they knew their saturation point. Rather than start splurging, they started saving. They increased their giving. They lived with less fear and more freedom. Just like Stephen Martin.

While poverty restricts freedom, wealth has the potential to bind as well. Mike Evans arrived at LaSalle after the check giveaway. A $500 check didn't prompt Mike's saturation point. Instead, it was the prospect of an eight-digit deposit to his bank account. The company he founded in his North Side apartment, GrubHub, became a 1,000-plus employee-strong business valued in the billions when it went public ten years later. After the initial public offering, Mike left the business and reaped the financial rewards from his decade of sweat equity.

While poverty restricts freedom, wealth has the potential to bind as well.

As his exit from the company approached, Mike began to plan for the substantial windfall he anticipated, making commitments in advance for how it would be allocated. In the ten years he grew the business, especially as it became increasingly successful, Mike watched how other people became affected by money, and in turn he became convicted of the need for intentionality when it came to his own finances. "When somebody gets cancer, we are quick to say we don't know the mind of God. When we struggle with tragedy, we ask, 'How am I supposed to respond?' The same is true for blessing," noted Mike. He couldn't wait until the saturation point arrived to know he had reached it. Mike had witnessed enough to know he'd likely fall into the trap of the ever-escalating financial security target. He needed to define contentment before a penny landed in his pocket.

> *"When we struggle with tragedy, we ask, 'How am I supposed to respond?' The same is true for blessing."*

Mike wanted to exercise a different muscle and to do so voluntarily, not involuntarily. When a windfall comes in, "it takes about three seconds before you start thinking about money" and how to protect the new gains, Mike reflected. The way to counteract the impulse? "The very first response has to be generosity." When generosity serves as our first response, we become vessels through which resources flow; we act as stewards, not owners. With repeated practice, we develop muscle memory, and generosity becomes the new reflex.

Stephen Martin, Kristen Metz, and Mike Evans occupy entirely different positions on the socioeconomic spectrum. But even though their vistas differ, they see abundance, enough, saturation. They've trained their vision outside the frame of scarcity, learning "the secret" of contentment, as Paul said. They've become reflexive givers.

....

When generosity serves as our first response, we become vessels through which resources flow; we act as stewards, not owners.

Determining a saturation point is a task for all of us, no matter where we land on the income-tax tables. We mark our saturation points because we recognize our own humanity. Even if our generosity muscles get plenty of exercise, we know how easily they can atrophy when we miss a workout. And it is work—hard work. We have to practice saying "Enough." Practice giving away our time, our love, our money, ourselves. Even with practice, we'll still sweat when we give. Just like our church sweated through the decision of how to spend the windfall. But the sweat, the sacrifice—that's what turns us into reflexive givers. And if you ask Stephen, Kristen, Mike, or any of the rest of us at LaSalle, we'd all respond that we wouldn't have it any other way.

III

THE GENEROUS LIFE

CHAPTER 7

LISTENING INSIDE OUT

Frankly, we were nervous on the Sunday of our check giveaway. It sounds righteous to give away five hundred dollars to every congregant in the church. But in practice, it scared all of us. We were holding $500 checks and feeling the weight of how to spend them responsibly. Some of us knew immediately what to do with the money. Others had a hunch or an idea. But the majority of us seemed to be expectantly open. We seemed to think a good idea and a clear direction were going to just come to us. We would simply "know" what to do.

Everywhere around us the ideas flew like popcorn kernels: *Ebola research! Foot care for the homeless! Art classes! Eyeglasses for the poor! Animal rescue! Scholarships for underserved communities!* While our amounts of money were modest, we felt like they could change the world. Simply by receiving the gift, we felt a particular sense of obligation to use it well, to leverage it as best we could. Since the instruction was to "do good with it," most of us wanted to do *the most good we could*. But how?

Almost immediately a few folks asked if they could simply give it back to the church. At first that comment sounded
like a lack of engagement, as if giving to the church was taking
the path of least resistance.
Come on! Dig deeper. You can
come up with something more
exciting than that! It didn't
take too much discussion,
however, before our opinions started to change (Was it fair
to judge another's generous instinct?) and returning the gifts
sounded reasonable, responsible, and exciting. How straight-
forward to just put our money back into circulation to feed the
hungry, supply the senior market, pay for kids' summer camp.
How profound as well. As one mother, Emily Yetter, put it so
beautifully:

Most of us wanted to do the most good we could. But how?

> We were well-intentioned with the plan of researching unique
> causes and how best to utilize every dollar. However, we have
> three children at home, ages 5 and under, and we both have
> rewarding and demanding careers outside the home. While
> the gifts have been on our minds constantly, we have not had
> time to consider our passions, focus on research, and connect
> as a couple to make a decision. However, we have continued
> to come back to our interest in benefiting our community. I
> have consciously considered the concept of "community"
> during our day-to-day routines. This led me to the answer.

It seemed obvious. The gift did not need to be used for some overly unique or sexy opportunity. It could be something that our family benefits from, that our family takes from, and that our family wants to give back to.

We choose to give to LaSalle Street Church! We choose to double the amount of the gift that you entrusted us with. We are thrilled at being able to give back to our church community at a magnitude that we would otherwise not have been able to consider!

To endorse the checks back to the church was not only a generous gesture but also a humble statement of solidarity and revealed a deep commitment to the everyday, ongoing, "regular" labor of the church. While we don't know for sure, as leaders we estimate almost forty people returned their money to the church or gave directly to church programs—approximately 13 percent of the recipients. Each dollar was appreciated and put to use immediately. Our budget was still in the red with only a few months left in the year, so those gifts enabled some of our programming to continue without interruption. And the givers were following a well-established truth that people give to what they know. Philanthropic research shows that people divide into two groups—those who give with their heart and those who give with their head. The ideal mix, of course, is when head and heart are in agreement—as they were in the Yetter family.

Many in the congregation had a direct sense of what they were called to do with their checks. Recent life experiences were pointing them onto a clear path. One of our seniors, Ruth Ann Webb, had recently lost her husband to a particularly aggressive tumor, and so she gave most of her money to brain cancer research. One woman who had recently buried her father gave her check to an assisted-living agency. Eight-year-old pet lover Mahalia White-Hodge rallied her Sunday school class to give money to a local animal shelter.

But what about the great undecided? How were the rest of us going to figure out what to do? We needed a way of listening to ourselves, to each other, and to the needs around us to discover how best to express our generosity.

By the following Sunday we had painted the lower level of our sanctuary with dry-erase paint. The saying "If these walls could talk" was coming to life before our eyes as stories appeared about Middle Eastern Bible smugglers, runaway youth, and medical doctors in the Congo. It was inspiring to learn about connections that fellow churchgoers had to efforts happening on almost all continents as well as throughout Chicago. Some of the messages posted were simply informational—the gifts were going to well-established agencies, and the givers just wanted

We needed a way of listening to ourselves, to each other, and to the needs around us to discover how best to express our generosity.

to inform the rest of us. Some of the newer plans, however, could only thrive with other churchgoers' support. These ideas were hunches, nudges of how to let love go in ways that solved a local challenge or met a community need.

In the weeks that followed, people wrote up their ideas, left their contact information, and began soliciting the undecided to their cause. While the campaigning was well-intentioned, a subtle kind of pressure began to seep into conversations. We needed a way of moving the ideas off the wall and into some facilitated dialogues where people could ask questions, study a budget, and make those head-and-heart connections. One such meeting was organized within the first month of the windfall: a dozen or so congregants presented and distributed materials about their proposals.

It was exhilarating to hear so many creative plans. Kristin Hu pitched an idea that was only going to take off if others came alongside her. Kristin teaches at a Chicago high school with a very large immigrant population. She had watched while high-performing students had been shut out of college opportunities because of their inability to apply for government-backed student loans. She hoped to create a scholarship fund that could assist these motivated students. Great idea. But unless others got on board, her solo five hundred dollars would do little to create the opportunities she was after.

Kristin was followed by Joy Miller, a passionate environmentalist with a big dream of a neighborhood green space.

For years we had hoped to construct a garden on the roof of our ministry building. We figured students from local schools could help tend the raised beds, the crops could be used in our Wednesday food programs, and it would simply be a responsible expression of citizenship. Joy's vision was larger. She had spent time visiting green roofs operated by Chicago chefs, she had interviewed contractors about building requirements and restaurant owners about purchasing the crops, and she had done a deep dive on crafting a budget.

In addition to Kristin's and Joy's pitches, we heard plans for an economic empowerment zone, a call to purchase a property where people could live in community, and an idea for offering low-interest business loans. All were wonderful. But we couldn't give to everything. AAUGH! Hearing about all these great causes made some of us feel pinched rather than lavishly free. Generosity was in danger of becoming, well, conflictual.

> Hearing about all these great causes made some of us feel pinched rather than lavishly free. Generosity was in danger of becoming, well, conflictual.

Is this what the generous life is all about? Feeling guilty about all those good causes you're *not* supporting, while at the same time justifying the projects you *are* supporting? And beyond the eagerness to solicit others to certain individual causes, we still needed to decide how the remaining money, the $1.4 million (what one senior called "The Big Money"), should be allocated. If our personal choices around the five hundred dollars were tense, what might happen when we started prioritizing the larger sum?

Drinking from a Fire Hose

It felt like a fast-moving, multidimensional train—the multiple interests, passions, and pulls we met in looking at giving. On some level, we began to feel like it was all a little too much. We had too much information, too many voices demanding our attention, too many needs coming in from all over the world—and too many decisions to make. We didn't think that taking generosity seriously was going to take so much time and so much energy. It felt like we were trying to drink from a fire hose. How would we ever be able to silence the external noise so we could better hear what the psalmist called "the desires of our heart"?

Silencing the noise—both literally and figuratively—isn't just the domain of generosity; it might be the prerequisite for intentional living. But it is one elusive animal that's getting increasingly difficult to find. Just the sheer amount of information we must wade

> We didn't think that taking generosity seriously was going to take so much time and so much energy. It felt like we were trying to drink from a fire hose.

through every day is stupefying. The Internet, smart phones, and 24-hour television give us *five times* the daily information individuals had in 1986. That's a staggering amount of information that we're busy reading, trying to use, and passing along to others. As USC professor Dr. Martin Hilbert puts it, "If a single star is a bit of information, there's a galaxy of information for every person on earth."[1]

Many of us are watching, listening, working, and consuming that onslaught of information at the same time we are eating our dinners, playing with our children, and meeting our friends. In a perverse way, trying to live more generously as a church was increasing our multitasking ways, as we struggled to add yet another thing to schedules and lives that were already on overload. We were having a difficult time judging right action from just action in general.

We were learning in real life what Stanford University professor Clifford Nass had learned in his research: that multitaskers are "suckers for irrelevancy." While we may think we can do several tasks at once, nimbly moving from text messaging to reading a recipe and from writing a business plan to checking the weather report, social science has proved otherwise. Studies show that people distracted by phone calls and emails experience a 10 percent drop in their IQ scores. Distressingly, the competency component that we're chasing is increasingly elusive, since our productivity decreases as much as 40 percent. And this is one situation in which practice does *not* make perfect. We don't get "better" at multitasking the more we do it; in fact, we simply become worse.[2]

We were those multitasking people! Trying to attend to more, more, more, even when it was keeping us from actually finding what we were seeking. But how could we possibly step back from this onslaught and find a place where we could listen from the inside out? Where we could gain a bit of perspective? An understanding of what the Jewish rabbis call *hakarat hatov*—of being able to recognize the good? A place of . . . dare we say it? *Wisdom.*

But how could we possibly step back from this onslaught and find a place where we could listen from the inside out? Where we could gain a bit of perspective?

Stepping Back

The great spiritual movements of the world have concerned themselves with this balance of living *in the world* while also experiencing a way of living *beyond the world*. In one of his more confusing observations, Jesus noted that his disciples were "not of the world, even as I am not of it" (John 17:16, NIV). Jesus didn't preach an escape-from-the-world theology; his life and death show a man clearly concerned with the needs and the joys of this life. Just the sheer number of dinners, parties, and weddings Jesus talked about indicate the deep pleasure he took in the celebratory events of our humanity. At the same time, he urged those around him to regularly pause, pray, and orient themselves to a world beyond this one. The apostle Paul teased out this teaching when he wrote to the Roman church, "Do not be conformed to this world, but be transformed by the renewing of your minds . . ." (Rom. 12:2). While we live in this world, we also embody an orientation of the world to come.

It's one thing to live untouched by the world in the first century. It's quite another when we've been drinking from a fire hose of information in the twenty-first century. Yet the antidote remains the same: Stop. Wait. Be still. Listen.

Mindfulness. Contemplation. Meditation. Silence. Prayer. These were the habits we LaSallers needed if we were going to get to the other side of generosity. We needed to find the deeper listening of the prophets, sages, and mystics. We wanted to use the kind of knowing long advanced by the philosophers—using our senses, carefully considering what made us passionate, thinking critically about the needs of the world, and taking a sober assessment of what could be accomplished—but we also sought guidance from beyond that way of knowing. We wanted a direction from outside ourselves. In religious terms, we sought the direction of God.

We needed to find the deeper listening of the prophets, sages, and mystics.

A kind of divine roadmap is what many of us seek, whether or not we use that language to describe it. It's difficult to get through a week or two without reading the story of a person who put their request out into the "universe" and received some sort of desired result. This is what Rhonda Byrne advocates in her bestselling book called *The Secret*. Simply put, the premise is that the universe rewards by giv-

We wanted a direction from outside ourselves. In religious terms, we sought the direction of God.

ing us those things we spend most of our time thinking about. There is a "law of attraction," Byrne says, and we pull the universe toward us by the kind of energy we put out into it. Think about how broke you are, for instance, and guess what? You attract the energy of poverty that is floating around in the universe. Better instead to think about possibilities and opportunities. That will allow the positive energy of good fortune to come your way. At best, this kind of "divine direction" is no more than confirmation bias that puts us at the center of our personal universe. At worst, this law of attraction mocks and distorts the real needs of poverty and want around the world.

We wanted nothing to do with this kind of divine direction. Rather, we were seeking some small echo of what some throughout Scripture experienced. Perhaps a path forward illuminated by a soft sign of a proverbial star, or something like a radiant bush, unusual enough that our attention would be piqued. Or even what the prophet Elijah sought when, in fear of his life and lacking any other option, he fled to a cave at Mount Sinai (1 Kings 19). Elijah stopped there. And waited. He waited

.... through the explosive thun-

We were seeking some small der of a lightning storm. He
echo of what some throughout waited through the destabi-
Scripture experienced. lizing force of hurricane-gale

winds. He waited through his hunger pains and self-directed solutions. He waited until he heard a *still, small voice*, as the text says. Then, he got up and acted.

When the news of our LoveLetGo campaign began to spread, emails, letters, packages, and photos from around the world began to accumulate in our church office. We got a large cardboard box to hold the manila envelopes, the CDs, and the posted letters. Then we got another one. Someone in South Carolina was facing foreclosure—they only needed thirty thousand to keep their home. Oh, and their husband was a disabled veteran as well. Another letter detailed a drug treatment center in danger of losing its funding. Surely we could spare one hundred thousand dollars to keep the clinic open? From throughout the country and around the world, the requests rushed in from people—some desperate and some politely interested—all wanting our money.

We read and answered every letter and email. We explained that we were putting every request aside while we stopped acting and started listening. Almost half of our congregation signed on to join a small group for reflection and prayer. Seventeen groups met at least once a month. We all read the same Scripture texts and discussed a similar set of questions. But that's where the similarities stopped. Some with heavy travel schedules or young children at home gathered around their cell phones for a conference call. Others met for a meal and several hours of active engagement. The modality was different, but the intention to hear the still, small voice was the same.

Prayer just doesn't need a lot of words.

Most of the great prayers are pretty simple. Jesus uses approximately thirty Aramaic words to give his disciples the *one prayer* that Christians have prayed virtually verbatim throughout the centuries (only 66 words in English). Meister Eckhart, a thirteenth-century philosopher and poet, once said, "If the only prayer you ever say in your entire life is thank you, it will be enough." There is wisdom in that sparse statement. Perhaps we have made prayer far more complicated than God intended it to be.

What prayer does need, however, is an awareness of the presence of God and an attentiveness to God's presence in the present moment.

Prayer just doesn't need a lot of words. Prayer doesn't need special phrases or words arranged in a particular order. What prayer does need, however, is an awareness of the presence of God and an attentiveness to God's presence in the present moment. That's why the first prayers of our community were rooted in something as simple as: Here. Now. Some of our prayer groups began in moments of silence. Or the leader might have read a Scripture verse such as Paul's statement in Acts 17:28, "In [God] we live and move and have our being," and then we would simply sit and drink in the truth of that reality. *Here* we are. *Now* in the presence of God's grace.

Here We Are

It's so easy to miss God when he shows up. One well-known story about mindfulness (told in Luke 10:38–42) recounts the time Jesus came to the home of two sisters, Mary and Martha. Jesus is traveling with an entourage of disciples, and Martha is the dutiful hostess—welcoming them, seeing that their feet are washed, attending to their needs, preparing the food. In short, she's doing all the things expected of women in that cultural setting. While her sister Mary simply ignores the social pressure, disregards all her expected responsibilities, and takes a seat right in front of Jesus. Perhaps almost daring someone to say something about it.

Martha is busy doing her job—her job as a woman in that

It's so easy to miss God when he shows up.

culture, her job as a homemaker, her job as a hostess. And not a person in that room likely would criticize her *for doing her job*. No one, that is, but Jesus, who realizes that the stress of her job is costing Martha her life.

Some have suggested that Jesus is critiquing a life of service—as if action and contemplation are so sharply divided that one is seen as better or holier than another. But that's a hard sell. Just before this scene Jesus told the story of the Good Samaritan, arguably one of his more memorable stories of caring for those around us. Instead, Jesus is criticizing the way that life—even really good life, with really good stuff—can make us distracted. *Periespato* is the Greek word for it. It's a word that means being pulled or dragged in different directions. Martha's distraction—*periespato*— gets in the way of her realizing that God is right here, in her midst. Sitting in her living room! This day that should be precious and treasured is flying by in a whirl of steamy cooking, dirty dishes, and growing resentment.

When Martha decides to get real by voicing her irritation in a public shaming of Mary, Jesus calmly and steadily redirects her energy. There's no screaming about whitewashed tombs and broods of vipers, no knocking over the tables to get her to see what's important. Jesus simply responds by drawing this exhausted, multitasking woman to her real self: *"Martha . . . Martha."* Jesus invites her beyond the many voices all needing attention and asks her to be present to the one thing necessary: sitting still and listening.

Mindfulness. Being here. Now. These are the starting points of transformational prayer. That's where we all must begin. It's the way through that deluge of information and multi-tasking. Stopping to say, *Here I am. Now.*

> Mindfulness. Being here. Now. These are the starting points of transformational prayer.

It's a practice God claimed as holy and good long before Martha's time. God invited people to take a regular day off—the Bible calls it a Sabbath—a day when one simply didn't cook or farm or make business decisions. One day that wasn't filled with grabbing information, curating our online image, and blogging about our political views. *Stop it!* God told the Hebrews. *Take a day off! Applaud your spouse for taking a nap on the sofa. Go swimming with your kids! Put down your to-do list and just enjoy the gifts all around you. I've created you to stop in the same way that I stopped from my own work.* Or, as Jesus soothingly invites, "Come unto me, and I will give you . . . " What? More work? No. Rest. "I will give you rest."

Slowly, hesitantly, many of us began to stop. We started to find some silence. And, ever so timidly, we entered into something we could describe as rest.

Recent research shows that chronic busyness is bad for our brains. Idle activities are those where our brains take a mental break. A real mental break—no watching television, playing video games, or scrolling through the news feeds—a break of nature walks, meditation, naps. Our brains must have idleness in order to function at capacity. In the same way necessary molecular and physiological processes occur

slowly, hesitantly, many of us began to stop. We started to find some silence. And, ever so timidly, we entered into something we could describe as rest.

primarily or only during sleep, so, too, some important mental processes seem to require times of idleness or daydreaming rest. "Being idle is one of the most important activities in life," writes Andrew Smart in his book *Autopilot: The Art and Science of Doing Nothing.*

The idleness research has led to an industry devoted to downtime as organizations across the board—Google, Coca-Cola, Ford, and Facebook, to name a few—use consultants like The Energy Project to teach their workers *how to not work.* But it's done more than that, too. As sloth has been praised as a means to greater productivity, new studies have begun asking just what sort of downtime is "the best"? Can we rank idle behaviors in terms of what we get out of them?

And this is where the research gets really interesting—especially for people of faith. Lo and behold, there are differences in the quality of downtime. While there are many different kinds of rest and types of idleness, the type of break that means the most is when we stop and experience awe. That's right: *Awe.*

Awe as in "an overwhelming feeling of reverence, admiration, or fear produced by that which is grand, sublime, extremely powerful, or the like." In other words, the most transformative rest we can have is that in which we are face-to-face with the eternal, the majestic, the glorious, the cosmic, the non-ending, always-beyond-us Mystery: what was going on in Martha's living room that day over two thousand years ago.

> *While there are many different kinds of rest and types of idleness, the type of break that means the most is when we stop and experience awe.*

The studies in awe started from a very practical place. Knowing that people were drinking from a fire hose, Stanford University professor Dr. Melanie Rudd and her team asked whether it was possible to alleviate the feeling that we never have enough time. Was there a way, they wondered, by which we could be freed from the sense that there is too little time available for all the things we need to do? That's when they discovered awe. Awe creates a sort of perceptual vastness—a plane of existence where we are aware of being part of something much larger than ourselves. This perceptual vastness in turn seems to trigger a desire in us to "accommodate" that vastness. Awe allows more beauty and wonder in our lives and makes us want to re-incorporate some of that new knowledge into our worldview.[3]

Throughout the centuries, the Bible has implored people to pause and stand in awe. The Psalms from beginning to end are rife with encouragement to consider the heavens, look at the fields, and exclaim the praises of God. Repeatedly we are admonished to *get our praise on.*

> Praise the LORD! Praise the LORD from the heavens; praise
>   him in the heights!
> Praise him, all his angels; praise him, all his host!
> Praise him, sun and moon; praise him, all you shining stars!
> Praise him, you highest heavens, and you waters above the
>   heavens!
> Let them praise the name of the LORD, for he commanded
>   and they were created. (Ps. 148:1–5)

Those admonitions to praise weren't for God's benefit; they were for our benefit. Practicing awe, just like practicing generosity, is simply good for us. We were created for it.

Practicing awe, just like practicing generosity, is simply good for us. We were created for it.

We LaSallers spent nine months gathering together. Every time we met, we had a window of awe. Sometimes it was in our opening psalm, read corporately or alone. Sometimes it was in our confession. Sometimes it was in our extended times of silence. But it was regular, purposeful, and expectant. We waited as Elijah had waited for the still, small voice. We looked in the way the magi looked for the star in the East.

And eventually we sensed there were a few burning bushes. There were a few ideas and projects that kept rising to the surface. Sometimes an idea that had started in one prayer school months earlier began to take on a level of importance across the church, or a project that initially had a lot of conviction would sputter and fade. We kept a record of those ideas that continued to appear. This was the starting point for our deeper analysis of generosity. After listening from the inside out, we were ready to listen from the outside in.

CHAPTER 8

LISTENING OUTSIDE IN

Like people across the country every morning, many LaSallers unwrap their local newspapers with a sense of dread. They anticipate stories of innocent children struck by stray bullets, impoverished communities plagued by endemic violence, and social service agencies hampered by state budget cuts. Add to that the national news headlines proclaiming shootings of unarmed black civilians, terrorist attacks prompted by hate, and the worst refugee crisis in modern history.

Some of us raise the white flag of surrender: the enormity of the problems defeats us. No matter what we do, suffering will continue to seep from every edge of the world. So we stop listening. Or we listen absent of hope.

Others of us choose to ignore the headlines, as if all the efforts we expend to orchestrate our lives will otherwise prove futile. Feeling threatened, we stop listening.

Others of us react still differently. Instead of ceasing to listen, we listen hard, but to only one thread of the web of information streaming toward us. We become single-issue soldiers, beating an activist drum and interpreting all other news through the lens of that single issue.

All of those reactions help us cope. Winnowing the voices from outside. Screening out what we have difficulty processing. Limiting what penetrates our minds and souls.

Deep down, we want to listen to all the voices. We were created to be social, empathic, other-oriented people. But we know we cannot process every single voice, we cannot address every ounce of pain and suffering, we cannot act as change agents for every worthy cause.

Just as we are called to practice listening inside out, we are called to practice listening outside in. Listening outside in, with intentionality and wisdom, becomes an exercise to fuel our generosity.

What *can* we do? Rather than ceasing to listen, or listening narrowly, or listening without hope, we can listen wisely, engage the needs of the world authentically, true to ourselves and to our generous instincts.

Just as we are called to practice listening inside out, we are called to practice listening outside in. Listening outside in, with intentionality and wisdom, becomes an exercise to fuel our generosity.

In Search of Big Ideas

After the excitement and media attention of the $500 check giveaway subsided, and we had listened inside out to discern how best to allocate that money, the church approached its next monumental task: to resolve how to allocate the remaining $1.4 million.

As you might suspect, literature on church leadership doesn't cover the topic of unexpected windfalls and how to distribute them. Across the country, only a handful of other churches had managed similar serendipitous events—not enough to draw any conclusions around a pattern of best practices. So LaSalle navigated new territory.

As you probably gathered from the stories shared thus far, LaSalle embraces an ethos of what one former pastor termed "every member ministry." Church members have a say in the church's direction. The vote in 1970 to invest in Atrium Village occurred after a Wednesday-night *worship service*, not a board meeting. Leaning toward democracy runs deep at LaSalle.

Democracy complicates decisions. Yet LaSalle's elders and leadership council committed to the principle of involvement from the start, regardless of the difficulties such a commitment might impose. And there were bound to be difficulties. How in the world do you get more than three hundred church members to agree on how to spend money? Our church needed a deliberate, thoughtful approach. We needed to listen wisely.

The chair of our council proposed that we conduct interviews to hear people's ideas on how to spend the money. But not your garden-variety, tick-the-box kinds of surveys. Instead, each interview began with basic questions about the person's history at LaSalle: what attracted them to the church, who in the church had influenced them, what kept them attending. Then the queries moved to key moments in their experience at LaSalle, with reflections on what those moments revealed about the church. Only at the end of the interview did we seek suggestions for how to spend the windfall, for the causes and concerns weighing on congregants' hearts. Listening attentively seeks more than answers; it searches for the journey to the answers.

We began the Big Idea interview process in earnest with the goal to conduct over one hundred interviews. To ensure that we reached every person and captured every thought, we also held a Big Idea mini-summit where church members could share their own ideas and hear others' ideas. We met in the same room where we had received our $500 checks only five months earlier. Dozens of people paraded across the podium to explain their hopes and dreams for the windfall. After combining like ideas together, we broke into small groups to begin turning ideas into outlines and plans—all

Listening attentively seeks more than answers; it searches for the journey to the answers.

captured on multi-colored, poster-size sheets that painted the beige walls by the end of the evening.

In our first leadership council meeting, we drafted a covenant: a promise to each other, to our church body, to our community, and to God. In the covenant we committed to listening to all voices, including the squeaky wheels (yes, churches have them), and especially to the quiet voices, the ones most likely to be disregarded or silenced in a systematic process.

Dan Price also chose to listen to voices unusual for him to hear under most circumstances. As CEO of Gravity Payments, Price's salary netted him over one million dollars a year. On a hike one day with a friend, Price listened as she shared a pressing burden: a $200 monthly rent increase she couldn't fathom accommodating. She earned $40,000 from her primary job and already accepted odd jobs on the side to supplement her income. Price's mental wheels started spinning. He promptly investigated the pay of his employees and learned that one-third of them received lower salaries than his friend.

He began to ask more questions. What he heard surprised him: "Some were living without running water. They were sleeping on friends' couches, commuting over an hour to work, waiting to start a family until they could afford it, and taking money out of their 401(k) to pay their bills."[1] In April of 2015 he announced he would raise the salaries of everyone at the company to a minimum of seventy thousand dollars. To fund the increase, Price would decrease his salary.

Detractors might suggest that savvy marketing strategy motivated Price more than generosity. But Price focused on two things: listening and keeping his word; Gravity's lowest-paid employees earn more now than they did. Price opened himself to understanding a financial reality he had left behind without looking back—until the day of his hike. After listening, intentionally and intently, he acknowledged the inequality between his pay and his employees' pay as "absurd." (Note: at twenty-five times the pay of a forty-thousand-dollar employee, Dan's "absurd" rate looked reasonably equitable compared to the average Fortune 500 CEO's pay, at 204 times that of the average employee.[2])

> *Listening wisely requires diverting our gaze to the expansive view, the bigger picture, the broader landscape.*

Remember WYSIATI: What you see is all there is? Listening wisely requires diverting our gaze to the expansive view, the bigger picture, the broader landscape. Price could have heard his friend's woes and written a story of scarcity with a predictable fairy-tale ending: *Compassionate wealthy friend provides desperately needed funds* or, better yet, *Benefactor writes blank check to friend threatened with homelessness.* Either action would merit a pat on the back. In Price's case, he saw not only his friend's predicament, but also the predicament of forty people whose lives *he could impact directly.* He saw a Big Idea in a small story. Listening wisely draws us away from the narrow outlines of the picture before us. In listening, we see more than what there is.

Open to Possibilities

Many biblical characters saw Big Ideas in small stories, despite the pragmatists and realists attempting to dissuade them. Every miracle required at least one person listening wisely, and others hoping expectantly. The healer and the healed both listened, open to possibilities beyond the visible frame of scarcity.

Like modern politicians on the campaign trail, Jesus and the disciples criss-crossed the landscape to spread the gospel message. Some scholars estimate that Jesus walked at least fifteen thousand miles in his thirty-some years, with several thousand of those miles logged during his active three-year ministry at the end of his life.[3] The first four books of the New Testament, collectively called the Gospels, record thirty-seven instances of Jesus performing miracles. If Jesus walked approximately three thousand miles during his active ministry and in that time stopped to perform miracles in thirty-seven locations, the math suggests an eighty-mile distance between miracles.

Granted, the site of every miracle may not be documented. Even doubling the number of places, the calculation returns an average forty-mile gap between miracles.

Walk forty miles from where you stand right now, in any

direction, and odds are you'll encounter more than one need for a miracle. Within forty *yards* of our church, we would likely stumble on several needs for a miracle.

Given the ground Jesus covered, why the apparent paucity of miracles? Did Jesus miss opportunities or fail to comprehend the needs around him? Seems unlikely, doesn't it?

Jesus listened, and listened wisely—*to those who trusted in what they could not see.* Miracles came to people who believed in miracles, who glimpsed a backdrop beyond scarcity's frame, who questioned the world's assumptions *and listened wisely* as Jesus responded. Miracles visited people open to possibilities.

> Jesus listened, and listened wisely—to those who trusted in what they could not see.

In the Gospel of Matthew, the residents of Nazareth provide an object lesson in how not to behave when the Son of God pays a visit (Matt. 13:54–58). When Jesus returns to his hometown of Nazareth and speaks in the synagogue, the crowd takes "offense" not at his teachings but at his perceived superiority. *This can't be the carpenter's son!* they mutter to each other. *We know his parents, his siblings . . . nothing special there. Where does he get off grandstanding in our synagogue?* They listened, but all the while wore their provincial blinders. The chapter closes, "And he did not do many deeds of power there, because of their unbelief." Jesus listened, but he couldn't hear anyone listening in return.

In the next chapter of Matthew, a mere thirteen verses later, Jesus encounters another crowd. This event occurs after Jesus practiced listening inside out—he returns from a solitary boat ride he took following the news of his cousin's death. His quiet, contemplative window slams shut as a "great crowd" greets him at the shore upon his arrival. People from nearby towns had heard that Jesus would be returning to shore, and they traveled by foot to see him, trickling in all day. Jesus spends the hours after his return healing the sick among the travelers. All in all, the sick and the well in the crowd number five thousand.

When evening approaches, the disciples begin to fidget. They understand crowd management and realize this crowd may start getting hungry—and ugly. They entreat Jesus to send the crowd into the villages to buy food. Jesus replies by instructing *them* to feed the crowd. Perhaps sarcastically, perhaps desperately, the disciples respond, "We have nothing here but five loaves and two fish." You may already know the ending: Jesus blesses the food and gives it to the disciples to distribute. All five thousand people in the crowd eat till they're content, and the leftovers fill twelve baskets.

Throughout the day, the disciples witnessed Jesus curing ailment after ailment. In their travels, they had seen Jesus cast out demons, return sight to the blind, even *raise a girl from the dead*. They had watched while Jesus challenged the wisdom and motives of powerful, respected religious leaders. Yet, this evening by the water, drowning in a sea of people, they see only five loaves and two fish.

What did the crowd see? The crowd, too, had witnessed Jesus's handiwork all day long. When Jesus told them to sit down, they listened. When he lifted the bread and the fish to heaven for a blessing, they listened. Without a notion of what might transpire, they listened expectantly, hopefully, trustingly.

When we listen to the deluge of bad news stories flooding in, what do we hear? The ticking of an antsy crowd ready to detonate like a time bomb? The faint thump of a meager five loaves and two fish as they drop into a basket? The screaming sweater of scarcity?

Listening wisely opens us to generosity—generosity expressed and generosity received. When we listen expectantly, we begin to conceive Big Ideas from small stories, like salary increases for forty people or five loaves feeding five thousand. Careful listening allows us to remember that there is a broader narrative in progress, and in our listening, we may even catch a glimpse of the role we have been asked to play.

Listening wisely opens us to generosity—generosity expressed and generosity received.

Filtering What We Hear

At our leadership council meeting following the Big Idea interviews and mini-summit, we were awash in data—spreadsheets, reports, anecdotes. Some of us questioned whether we had listened so wisely after all! Others of us secretly wished our elder board had decreed what the church would do with the funds, to save all the time, effort, and discernment ahead.

What frame, what construct would accommodate the overflowing Big Idea information?

Only a frame where listening inside out and listening outside in could intersect. Like merging galaxies, LaSalle's identity (inside out) and a Big Idea (outside in) could orbit closer and closer together until they formed an immense constellation, illuminating the previously murky space. Generosity acts like the gravity drawing the galaxies together, triggering a release of explosive energy when ideas and identity unite.

In LaSalle's solar system, Jesus clearly acted as our sun, sustaining life and pulling us near. What served as our planets? Our moons? Without knowing ourselves, we would fail to interpret the interstellar radio messages coming to us in the form of proposals from the congregation. Listening outside in required understanding LaSalle from the inside out.

The leadership council created a group of trees, with each tree representing a compilation of ideas sharing a common theme, or trunk. One tree trunk symbolized the local neighborhood, another our global neighbors. In total our church had five different trees, but *each tree grew from identical roots*. LaSalle's core identity formed those roots: commitment to faith, social justice, and advocacy.

Listening wisely first requires openness. Second, it requires filtering information through the screen of identity. Without filters, we run for cover from the barrage of information aimed at our heads and hearts. At our church we recognized our passions, our talents, and our resources. In doing so, we could discern the presence of a spark when a Big Idea lit up an aspect of our identity. Filters allow our core selves—as individuals or as an institution—to respond authentically and lavishly to the needs we were designed uniquely to fulfill.

Filters allow our core selves—as individuals or as an institution—to respond authentically and lavishly to the needs we were designed uniquely to fulfill.

Unique. Every person. Every person possesses a set of stories and a point of view exclusively their own. Though you may take in the same barrage of information as the person next door, you will experience every word and image differently:

> Now there are varieties of gifts, but the same Spirit; and there are varieties of services, but the same Lord; and there are varieties of activities, but it is the same God who activates all of them in everyone. . . . All these are activated by one and the same Spirit, *who allots to each one individually just as the Spirit chooses.* (1 Cor. 12:4-6, 11; emphasis added)

Filtering allows us to answer the calls intended for our

ears. We still hear the other cries—the ones breaking both our hearts and the heart of the Creator. But we trust those cries to be heard by the people meant to respond. Our world holds plenty of cast members for the dramas unfolding.

The sweet spot of generosity comes at the congruence of identity and unmet needs. Listening outside in hinges on the work of listening inside out. The two practices meet and intertwine, and in the choreography, Big Ideas emerge from small stories. Or, as writer and theologian Frederick Buechner affirms, "The place God calls you to is the place where your deep gladness and the world's deep hunger meet."[4] Using these practices, we get a hunch about where our story fits into the grander narrative. But how do we know our hunch is correct? Only by taking the first steps.

> *The sweet spot of generosity comes at the congruence of identity and unmet needs. Listening outside in hinges on the work of listening inside out. The two practices meet and intertwine, and in the choreography, Big Ideas emerge from small stories.*

Learning to Dance

Have you ever tried learning to ballroom dance? Finding our own feet, much less navigating our partner's, proves tricky. The glorious music begins, we grasp our partner's hand, then proceed to fumble the first few—or several—times through. The give-and-take between partners, the negotiating of each other's inclinations, the leaning in and pushing back—all become part of the journey to generosity. Remember the interplay between Dan West and the worker at the daycare center? They listened carefully to the music, tripped over each other's feet for a spell, and at last found their rhythm.

Listening wisely requires openness, filters, and finally, a willingness to learn to dance.

People learn to dance every day in their respective fields, whether in business, religion, academia, science, or government. They regularly explore new environments, new data, new ideas. To interpret the newness, they follow a common approach: develop a hypothesis, test the hypothesis, draw a conclusion. Researchers repeat the method until they land on a valuable insight, with each interim conclusion winnowing their hypotheses and at the same time expanding their knowledge.

Listening wisely requires openness, filters, and finally, a willingness to learn to dance.

Generosity's dance plays out similarly. We listen outside in, open to seeing a Big Idea in a small story. We filter out the needs designed for others to address, focusing on our particular role in the stories written for us. We hypothesize how we might alter the plot of the story. Then we take our first dance steps.

Two of our congregants, Paul Hettinga and Larry Reed, have finely honed business and financial acumen from their successful careers. Both possess keen listening skills and entrepreneurial instincts. And both recognize that their success depended upon people, opportunities, and resources that less educated, poorer people cannot access. For years, Paul and Larry would talk periodically about the inequality they witnessed in Chicago, especially among the people whom LaSalle's ministries served.

After receiving their $500 checks, Paul and Larry sensed they needed to move from talking about the topic to acting on it. But what would action look like? Unequal access to resources involved a host of issues: sparse financial capital for entrepreneurs without a track record, the vicious cycle of the payday loan model, lack of affordable childcare for people trying to gain job skills or attend school, legal hurdles to clearing the records of people who made a single mistake for which they still paid decades later—among a laundry list of other barriers.

Larry's experience in microfinance made him an expert on assessing risk. Paul's management experience had given him coaching and nurturing skills. As leaders in their organizations, they both could cast visions for the future and mark a path to reach it. Knowing themselves, they determined their first dance steps: to use their $500 checks as seed money for what they would call the Dream Fund. The fund would provide microloans to local entrepreneurs lacking access to capital, and would be accompanied by mentorship from Paul, Larry, and anyone else at LaSalle who volunteered.

Soon Paul and Larry asked other congregants to deposit their checks into the Dream Fund. They also invited others to help define how the Dream Fund could be part of a multi-pronged strategy for improving the financial health of LaSalle's neighbors, including alternatives to payday loans, job training, financial counseling, and childcare networks. By the time the Big Idea interviews commenced, the Dream Fund had evolved into a vision of an economic empowerment zone, a four-block radius around LaSalle where every resident would have access to the kinds of resources Paul and Larry had during their careers. Talk about a Big Idea!

For every Big Idea consistent with LaSalle's identity, at least one person on the leadership council was assigned to speak in depth with the idea's promoters. This liaison's task was to understand the idea, think through the implementation process, project its potential impact, and also pray for and support these congregants sticking their necks out in response to some nudge or call they discerned. As Paul and Larry went through the process, they disproved two of their initial hypotheses. Budding entrepreneurs from disadvantaged backgrounds had access to funds—plenty of secular and government programs offered money, and those organizations provided mentorship and coaching as well. They also came to realize that the level of human resources required to put an empowerment zone in place far eclipsed the volunteer capacity available at LaSalle. Even though they anticipated devoting themselves at a near full-time level, their hours couldn't sustain a program of such broad reach and vision.

Paul and Larry could have stopped moving. Turned off the music and walked away. But they continued to hear the sounds of a call and wanted to learn the dance steps. Then a new partner appeared in the reception hall.

In the 1960s, the church birthed the first faith-based legal aid clinic in the country, Cabrini-Green Legal Aid (CGLA). The ministry had thrived, and continued to serve thousands of Chicagoans with legal advice and representation. Many of CGLA's clients were exactly the people Paul and Larry had in mind when envisioning the empowerment zone: young parents who couldn't afford childcare while they went to classes, potential entrepreneurs who had no collateral to secure a loan, people whose single marks on their criminal records prevented them from getting jobs. What about starting with these folks, understanding their most pressing needs, and figuring out which parts of an empowerment zone could be managed by a combination of volunteers and a dedicated staff person at CGLA?

It wasn't the dance Paul and Larry or the people who rallied around them envisioned. But they kept dancing, and in a way that reflected their unique abilities and personalities. "It will have its proper birth. I love the idea, and I've come to understand how much I love business. It involves everything:

economics, training, nurturing, caring for people, providing," Paul reflected. To Paul, the idea of dedicating himself to improving the financial wellness of people who lack resources felt natural: "It's not a big deal. Because my whole life has kind of been preparation. It feels like I am just being me."

When we live into our giver identities, we remember our framing story of abundance. We recognize our part in a bigger story. And instead of tuning out the barrage of bad news, we listen closely. Challenges that appear insurmountable become "not a big deal" because we know ourselves and our abilities, and we rest assured that others who know themselves will listen, too. Listening wisely, reflecting on our identities, and hypothesizing solutions together prepare us for action. At LaSalle, these practices guided us in choosing which of the Big Ideas truly sang to our collective body of skills and passions and energies. Then, when the doors opened and generosity invited us to dance, we responded with a joyous, grateful, and resounding Yes!

> When we live into our giver identities, we remember our framing story of abundance. We recognize our part in a bigger story.

This is our story, as we've said before, but it can be your story, too.

CHAPTER 9

REFRAMING THANKFULNESS

Say thank you. *For what?* you might ask. For anything. For everything, really. Saying thanks is one of the greatest gifts we can give ourselves. The studies on thankfulness reveal the same pattern we looked at in Chapter Seven on generosity. According to a 2003 study from Stanford University, keeping a gratitude journal gives us more restful sleep and less physical pain.[1] Saying thanks lowers our blood pressure and cuts our risk for depression by a third. And as your mother always said, saying thanks is good for our careers. Gratitude helps us achieve our professional goals and make better decisions. Most striking of all, gratitude affects our ability to forgive others who have wronged us.[2] Grateful people are more likely to respond with mercy rather than vengeance when they are wronged. Since grateful people see themselves as more connected with those around them, they have a greater sense of empathy. Gratitude not only improves our lives; the accumulated effect of gratitude may even prolong our lives as well.

Like generosity, gratitude is a super-power.

What we saw at LaSalle was how often people gave money to others as a way of saying thanks. Recent studies in neuro-science prove this connection as well. Brain scans show that activating the gratitude side of our brain fires up the generos-ity side of our brain. And vice-versa. Gratitude and generosity work in tandem.

Johanna Thompson understands this interplay between gratitude and generosity. Several years ago, during a sermon series on stewardship, people at our church shared their giv-ing stories. Johanna's story stayed with many of us be-cause it spoke deeply to our own experience:

Like generosity, gratitude is a super-power.

> I started giving because one day I realized I believe in this church. Because I get so much more back than I give. . . . I realized I wanted to be deliberate about tithing, really tithing, to this little church family that saved me by being Jesus all day, that is full of beautiful disasters, just like me. I wanted to tithe because I was floored by the financial generosity I saw in this little family of beautiful disasters.

Saying thanks by giving something of value has a long his-tory throughout Scripture. The biblical writers knew that what we choose to give reveals something about the disposition of

our hearts. Recall the story of King David from Chapter Five:
God blesses David with vast resources and immense power, but
the King starts to believe he
has created it all by himself.

> *Saying thanks by giving something of value has a long history throughout Scripture.*

When David comes to his
senses (in a dramatic story
you can read in 2 Samuel 24),
his first act is to say thank you
by building a monument—an altar—to God. A local wealthy
man, Araunah, hears that David is seeking a field and materials
for the monument and offers his own resources. *Here, take my
barn, my wood, my animals, dear King! You don't have to spend
your own money.* But David declines. During his rich and eventful life, he has learned that his whole life has been a gift, and
he wants to say thank you in a way that means something to
him: "'I will not offer burnt offerings to the LORD my God that
cost me nothing.' So David bought the threshing floor and the
oxen for fifty shekels of silver. David built there an altar to the
LORD, and offered burnt offerings and offerings of well-being"
(2 Sam. 24:24–25).

David didn't want to use the rich man's resources as if they
were his own. He wanted to say thank you by giving something
he valued and treasured. *I will not sacrifice something that cost
me nothing!*

Isn't that the way it is with us? We want to tell others
"Thank you" in a way that shows them how much they mean

to us. We've received something of value, and we want to say thanks by giving something of similar value.

As LaSalle discussed what we should do with the remaining $1.4 million, it became clear to us that we needed to express our solidarity with and gratitude for people around the city who were engaged in the kind of work that had led to Atrium Village in the first place. We wanted others to experience the surprising joy and freedom LaSalle had felt with the windfall. So we allocated another 10 percent, $160,000, to just give away to Chicago churches and agencies that were engaged in community building and justice work.

We want to tell others "Thank you" in a way that shows them how much they mean to us.

There would be no application process or hoops to jump through. Through our long engagement with the city, we had come across plenty of amazing leaders and groups. Some were people who wondered if they were making a difference. They had spent decades fighting for the same cause: using their money to rent vans for summer camps, or buying groceries and sheltering homeless high school students through important exam weeks. Others wondered if anyone outside their neighborhood even noticed them and the value of their work. It was impossible for us to acknowledge all these generous people. But at least some would soon find checks in the mailbox with notes that said simply, *You are making the world a better place. Thanks.*

The Echo of Gratitude

Not only do tangible acts of gratitude connect us to the present, but expressing thankfulness has a way of grounding us to the past and projecting us into the future. An act of grateful thankfulness can span the years and connect people in ways we can scarcely imagine.

When King David is at the end of his life—he has reigned for forty years—an entire generation has known only him as king. David's son, Solomon, will succeed him. Yet Solomon as described in 1 Chronicles 29:1 is "young and inexperienced" and facing a great task, according to his father. It is a fragile and vulnerable time for the country. Another king might have used the time to fortify his borders, build up his army, and consolidate his family's power.

Expressing thankfulness has a way of grounding us to the past and projecting us into the future. An act of grateful thankfulness can span the years and connect people in ways we can scarcely imagine.

But instead the aging king's last act on earth is planning to build a temple to the Lord as an expression of gratitude.

This is no weak-kneed, coerced act of generosity. The text says David is downright overwhelmed that he has the opportunity to say thanks in such a grand way. "Who am I, and what is my people, that we should be able to make this freewill offering? . . . For we are aliens and transients before you . . . ; our days on the earth are like a shadow . . ." (1 Chron. 29:14-15).

David's *thank you* carried weight. His action helped define the Israelites' national identity. Gratitude described who they were as people. At LaSalle we came across many others who also defined their lives by thanksgiving. Almost fifteen years ago Jessica Young taught dance at a small school housed in Atrium Village. She became fast friends with elementary teacher Lieschen Llerena Ridgeway. At the age of thirty-two, Lieschen was diagnosed with thyroid cancer. She achieved full remission after a several-year fight, during which time she married and enjoyed what many of us take for granted: our health. Lieschen never lost the wonder of how good it is to just be alive. She held annual gratitude parties for her friends to celebrate their many blessings.

Then, at the age of forty, a new cancer appeared, this time in her colon. The prognosis was bleak. Throughout the next four years of treatment, Lieschen never stopped being grateful for the day at hand. In fact, for the last two and a half years of her life, Lieschen kept a *daily account* of what she was thankful for. Posting on her Facebook page, late at night after the bustle of treatments and lab work was done, she was clear and specific: the song of an early bluejay, a Cubs victory, a note from a friend. On Day 842, well after midnight, Lieschen wrote: *I am thankful I saw the sunlight today. The next few days call for clouds.*

It would be her last entry.

Lieschen died on Day 848, February 29, 2016. She was forty-four years old.

At her memorial service, her family requested that everyone in attendance find a reason to thank someone every single day. Saying thanks was the best way they could imagine to honor this woman who lived each day with a full heart of gratitude. Jessica responded to her friend's life and death by choreographing and performing a dance in Lieschen's honor. It was a dance infused with the wonder of life.

Gratitude isn't contained by the present moment. It reverberates from year to year and from person to person. If we pause for a moment, each of us can likely see how much our lives have been blessed by others. Consider this example from LaSaller Becky Haase. For decades Becky and her husband, Jerry, have lived modestly and given extravagantly. When asked about the motivation behind her generosity, Becky had this to say:

The years 1952 and 1953 were bad years for my family. My father suffered a massive heart attack from which he never really recovered. He spent nearly 6 months of those two years in the hospital. Then I developed pneumonia and had a catastrophic reaction to peni-

Gratitude isn't contained by the present moment. It reverberates from year to year and from person to person.

cillin. I spent 6 weeks in the hospital and the entire summer of 1953 slowly regaining my strength. By Christmas of 1953 my family was broke and very nearly homeless. Yet that year I received three presents that had a tremendous effect on me. One was a "gently used" dime store doll nicely wrapped and provided by the Salvation Army at Christmas. One was the gift of 6 pints of blood donated by Masonic "brothers" of my father during my hospitalization. (There were no blood banks in 1953.) And the last was the gift of a year's worth of ballet and acrobatic lessons (possibly provided by a farmer who lived near us—no one ever knew) to help me recover. The doll and the year of ballet taught me to always give gifts that I would want to receive or that I would want to give to my own child. . . . The gift of blood and the year of ballet taught me that you can never even hope to repay a gift no matter how hard you try. You can only accept graciously and pass on to others whatever you can to ease someone else's life.

From one to another we pass on echoes of generosity.

Practicing Thankfulness: The Big Reward

In his book *Outliers*, Malcolm Gladwell tells the memorable story about the Beatles and their pre-fame days of playing at a strip club in Hamburg, Germany. There, the Fab Four played eight-hour sets, seven days a week, for months at a time. Most Beatles experts agree that without that time of intense, repeated practice, the Beatles never would have hit the radar. In Gladwell's summary, "Practice isn't the thing you do once you're good. It's the thing you do that makes you good."[3]

The very word "practice" may remind you of piano lessons and grueling after-school sport workouts. But we practice our way into all sorts of behaviors and characteristics. We learn bravery and courage, for instance. Former Boston College professor and theologian Mary Daly is often quoted on this subject: "Courage is . . . a habit, a virtue: You get it by courageous acts. It's like you learn to swim by swimming. You learn courage by couraging."[4]

Similarly, practicing thankfulness is a learned behavior. We learn thankfulness by thanking. That's what those gratitude journals are all about. It's the ongoing habit of naming our blessings on a regular basis—daily or weekly—that leads to the benefits of better health, deeper sleep, and greater connectedness with others. Connecting thankfulness with generous giving works the same way. It takes some effort, as Johanna learned: "I realized I wanted to *be deliberate*." But the reward is ultimately the thing most of us crave almost more than anything: freedom.

> *Practicing thankfulness is a learned behavior.*

Throughout this book we've tied generosity to a way of living that is freeing. We've used the word deliberately because that's how people describe what generosity has meant to them. There is a sense of contentment, a thread of connectedness, a joy and a peace that have rooted themselves into the soil of their lives. All together it adds up to freedom.

Freedom is what God has always desired for us. But we practice ourselves into freedom in the same way we practice ourselves into thankfulness. In Chapter Six we discussed the importance of knowing when enough is enough. There is a "saturation point" for acquisitions—after which having more stuff doesn't mean having more happiness. Finding that saturation point was one of the lessons of the long sojourn through the wilderness. The Israelites were no longer in physical bondage. But being liberated didn't necessarily make them free. Freedom was something they had to learn. They weren't going to learn freedom by simply hearing the story about it (though recounting the story was important). Instead, they were going to learn how to be free by learning how to handle the blessings they had been given. True freedom carried with it some disciplines, some habits. God was going to take care of them every day by providing quail and manna. But in response they were to take

> *Freedom is what God has always desired for us. But we practice ourselves into freedom in the same way we practice ourselves into thankfulness.*

only what they needed for that day and to trust that what they needed tomorrow would be there as well. If they tried to take too much, the food would rot in their hands. It would upset their stomachs. It would begin breeding maggots.

Could the people hold the gifts of God loosely? Trusting God and trusting each other? In other words, could the Israelites live as free people in the land of freedom? Or had they just traded one form of slavery for another? It's a good question for us, too.

When LaSalle started giving away the remaining $1.4 million, someone described it as living "fearlessly." One LaSaller realized that LoveLetGo was about far more than money:

> For me, generosity is about letting go of all that I'm holding on to. Sure, that's money. But it's also all the illusions I hold on to as well. For instance, I practice generosity at work when I give everything I have to help somebody organize their thoughts or break free from an addiction or whatever. I leave it all on the field. And yet at the very same time, I'm free from the outcomes. Generosity allows me to move past the feeling that they MUST get better in order for my efforts to mean something. When I'm generous I'm stepping out of the game of acquiring and achieving

You and I make all sorts of decisions that we think are going to free us—but instead they so easily become a different way of making us slaves again. To worry. Or debt. Or consumption. Or ease. And we often choose to be enslaved to the need to control or to maintain power or appearances.

The Sinai desert wasn't the only time God gave the Israelites the manna test. As they camped on the edge of the Promised Land, they heard the same warning again:

....

You and I make all sorts of decisions that we think are going to free us—but instead they so easily become a different way of making us slaves again.

The LORD your God is bringing you into a good land ... with flowing streams, with springs and underground waters welling up in valleys and hills, a land of wheat and barley, of vines and fig trees and pomegranates, a land of olive trees and honey, a land where you may eat bread without scarcity, where you will lack nothing, a land whose stones are iron and from whose hills you may mine copper. ... Take care that you do not forget the LORD your God, by failing to keep his commandments. (Deut. 8:7-9, 11)

Translation: The place you are going to dwell is awesome. Amazing. Where you are going to till the soil and create beauty, where you will put down roots and establish professions. But take care! Don't forget these are blessings. Use them as God has established them to be used. Treat them as God has commanded they be treated. Don't forget!

But we do forget. We forget because we can't smell the rotting manna. We forget because we don't see the way the blessings have become chains of a different sort. We forget because we don't practice living as free people.

What we've seen throughout our experience at LaSalle Street Church—and what we've shown you throughout this book—is that there is a way of living freely and openly with yourself, with others, and with God. Essentially it comes down to what habits you are going to form. And what way of life you are going to practice.

As Johanna found out when she started the habit of generosity, you won't experience magic, but you will experience the miraculous:

> One last note: I didn't become miraculously rich because I started giving more to God. I didn't win the lotto, didn't get an extremely lucrative raise. But here's the part that I do find sort of miraculous: I don't miss the money. Money's still tight, but no more so than before. I feel richer, though. I find myself deeply embraced in a culture of generosity. . . . I give, I receive, I give, I receive. Sometimes money, sometimes prayer, sometimes love, sometimes a shot of honesty, but it's a cycle of giving that has meaning. And I notice I have an attitude of giving more in other parts of my life and this makes me less of

a jerk most days. Is this a miracle? I don't know about miracles so much. I do know that sometimes it takes an act of God to get me to change, though . . . so, well . . . there's that.

This is a thankful person. Thankful people realize they live in a world of interconnected blessings. They know that the good they do is an echo of the good done to them. They realize the rich interplay of giving and receiving and no longer have to hold anything—even life itself—so tightly. They practice thankfulness, and in so doing they become just what God always intended them to be: free.

> *Thankful people realize they live in a world of interconnected blessings. They know that the good they do is an echo of the good done to them.*

Like Johanna and Becky and Lieschen, LaSalle as a church body practiced gratitude during the nine-month discernment process. We recounted our blessings around the table in our "fish schools." We reviewed the day's gifts in our prayers. We fasted and remembered the simple pleasure of a bite of bread. We handed over five hundred dollars to people and causes far and wide, feeling privileged and grateful to do so. And at the end of the process we gave away more: the majority of the $1.4 million windfall. We had no interest in hoarding the manna. LaSalle had practiced its way into generosity—and freedom.

CHAPTER 10

LETTING LOVE GO

Remember how you felt the last time you heard a story of generosity? Perhaps it was the story of a stranger who paid the bus fare for someone short on change, or a community coming alongside a wounded war veteran, or a teacher who changed the trajectory of a student's life. Remember your smile of surprise? The quick tears that welled up in your eyes? The sense of happiness that filled your heart? That hopeful conviction that the world is going to be okay?

Witnessing the generous act of just one person makes the world bigger somehow. Possibilities start to emerge.

If so, you're not alone. Many of us feel the same way. Witnessing the generous act of just one person makes the world bigger somehow. Possibilities start to emerge. We find in one small story the hint of a larger story at play. In the moment, we have little trouble escalating up from the solitary sound-bite of a news item to a world renewed by faith and generosity.

For most of us, though, the feeling fades pretty quickly most of the time. Because the next sound bite reminds us of the obstacles in the way. Famine in war-torn Syria. Wildfires in California. An ISIS attack in Paris. We are yanked from the plane of generosity as if tethered by the ankle to earth, reeled in by the pull of earthly problems.

Yet some people cling to hope. The feeling of possibility lingers. And they move in the direction of promise.

Just like two people at St. Paul's United Church of Christ, located a quick drive northwest of our church. After hearing about LaSalle's LoveLetGo campaign, two members approached their senior pastor with an idea: Could they donate $50,000 to the church and have the church distribute $500 checks randomly to one hundred of its households? The donation became their church's version of Atrium Village—a surprise windfall with no logical explanation and no one to thank but God, as the two donors chose to remain anonymous.

When the pastor announced the gift on a spring morning, he preached about Jesus calling Simon and Andrew as they sat in their boat while fishing on the Sea of Galilee. Jesus issued a direct and simple call to the brothers: "Follow me and I will make you fish for people" (Matt. 4:19). The text in both Mark and Matthew tells us that Simon and Andrew immediately left their nets and followed Jesus. *Immediately*. Without hesitation. Without debate. They heard the call and answered it.

The pastor reminded the congregation that St. Paul's had

been listening to and following a call for nearly 175 years. Those two congregants who donated simply reflected a body of believers all striving to get out of their boats and walk toward Jesus. For almost two centuries—almost as long as the city of Chicago had been incorporated—the church had been making a joyful noise, sharing the good news of the gospel. With their checks, St. Paul's congregants would "Repeat the Sounding Joy," as they titled their campaign, continuing to spread hope, possibility, and promise in a world in need of good news.

Jenny Brandhorst, a former LaSaller who now attends St. Paul's, received one of the randomly allocated checks. As a person who has supported many causes, she seriously deliberated which cause to choose. In the end, she gave her random windfall to a child whose life revolves around random acts of kindness.

At age four, Jaxton Engstrom was a happy, healthy little boy like any other preschooler. By age five, his eyesight had deteriorated to the point where he couldn't recognize family members in pictures. Within a few more years, Jaxton's speech and sleep habits changed, and he began to have seizures. One week before his seventh birthday, Jaxton was diagnosed with a rare and fatal genetic disease.

While Jenny felt helpless after first hearing Jaxton's story, she also felt inspired by this young boy. As a Dr. Seuss fan who loves *How the Grinch Stole Christmas*, nine-year-old Jaxton has one goal: to help the Grinch's heart grow bigger. How? By encouraging people to perform random acts of kindness and then by recording their acts on paper hearts they send to him. Jaxton collects these hearts, and though he cannot see them, he can count them, feel them, and sense the Grinch's heart expanding with each piece of paper.

Jenny wanted to celebrate this boy whose vast heart collection mirrors the depth of his own heart. So, enlisting the help of Jaxton's principal, teacher, and many others (including the Grinch!), Jenny arranged for a surprise party at Jaxton's school, where he received her $500 check and a note translated into Braille. "I know God's hands were everywhere throughout the process," said Jenny.

The sounding joy repeated and repeated—from the two people who heard a call and spoke to their pastor, to the pastor and church leaders who said yes to an idea. From Jenny receiving one of the random $500 checks, to an eight-year-old boy who can't see but can hear the abundance of joyful noise he creates, one heart at a time. Every one of them had let love go.

Gifts—passed along from one to another—transform the world.

Gifts—passed along from one to another—transform the world. No one knew that truth better than the apostle Paul. Decades after the first disciples heard and followed the call of Jesus, the apostle Paul leans back in a Roman jail cell and marvels at how God's message, called *the good news*, is spreading throughout the known world. And much of it is happening *without him*. "The Message is as true among you today as when you first heard it. It doesn't diminish or weaken over time. It's the same all over the world. The Message bears fruit and gets larger and stronger, just as it has in you.... It's as vigorous in you now as when you learned it from our friend and close associate Epaphras" (Col. 1:5–8, *The Message* translation).

Here's Paul, the self-proclaimed apostle to the Gentiles, encouraging a little band of followers he likely never met, living in a city he likely never visited. The church in Colossae (modern-day Turkey) was birthed not by Paul's letter or the preaching of John or Peter or any other "famous" disciple. Instead, a local guy named Epaphras spoke. And the people believed. And they started living the message. They bore fruit.

The message of God's generosity is the same all over the world. And at all times and in all places some have chosen to echo that message with acts of their own. And by their acts, the message bears fruit. The sounding joy repeats. The love is let go—by the guy down the street, nine-year-old boys, anonymous benefactors, and people like you and me.

The message of God's generosity is the same all over the world.

At the Shoreline

Since the LoveLetGo campaign started, we've heard from churches and schools around the country that decided to live generously by distributing checks to their members along the lines of LaSalle. But generosity doesn't require a formal community. All that's required is an openness to listening and a willingness to engage. That's it. You don't need to have the heart of a saint; you already have a giver's heart. You don't need a hefty bank balance; you already live in a world of abundance. You don't need to develop a particular talent or skill; you've already been given a role to play in the grand narrative of generosity.

Generosity doesn't require a formal community. All that's required is an openness to listening and a willingness to engage.

So where do you begin? May we suggest at the shoreline.

Earlier in the book we looked at the miracle Jesus performed in feeding a crowd of five thousand with five loaves and two fish. This miracle stands as the *only* miracle recorded in all of the Four Gospels. Clearly, God has a message for us within this story. In Chapter Eight, we understood that part of the message is a need to be open to possibilities—to have faith in the plausibility of miracles. But in this moment on the shoreline, we can gain deeper insight into generosity.

The disciples come to Jesus stressed and anxious about

the gathered crowd and limited food, and when they ask him to do something about the presenting problem, he tosses the hot potato back, telling them to feed the masses. The disciples are in no position to accomplish this task; after all, as itinerant ministers, they depend on other people to provide their food, shelter, and clothing! We understand the disciples' skepticism in the moment. Jesus's response to their incredulity is to ask, "How many loaves have you?" (Mark 6:38).

How many loaves have you, disciples? How many loaves have *you*? You, Bob. You, Sally. You, Manuel. You, Shanice. *You.* What do *you* have? What resources sit at your disposal? What characteristics do you possess to solve this problem? That's the beginning. That's where generosity starts. With where you are and who you are right now, at this very moment. We don't need to worry about what we don't have. Because God's got that covered.

> *That's where generosity starts. With where you are and who you are right now, at this very moment.*

What have you been hearing lately? What stories have caught in your throat recently? Who in your circle has crossed your mind when you allowed your thoughts to wander? These are the clues, the hints God offers. Starting with what you know.

Chris Ford knows football. This long-time LaSaller lived the gridiron life in high school and college. When he received his $500 check, he had been volunteering for several months as the linebacker coach for a school in the North Lawndale neighborhood, an area typically ranking in the top three of Chicago neighborhoods for crime. In the late fall, at the end of the football season, the team had qualified for the playoffs and finished second in its conference—no small victory for students up against much more than the physical prowess of the opposing team.

Despite coming from a background entirely different from that of the players, Chris earned their trust. As the team's head coach, Z. Johnson, said, "So many of our guys are yelled at, cussed at, screamed at every day. [Chris] speaks [of] life."[1] Of life beyond street corners run by gangs. Of life outside the broken families and broken systems meant to support those families. Of life bigger than the statistics showing that one-third of black males born today will spend time in prison.[2] Chris knew football, and from raising his own children, he knew these kids needed faith in something bigger than he could deliver in a single season.

So Chris used his $500 LoveLetGo check to start a chapter of the Fellowship of Christian Athletes (FCA).[3] To provide a place for these guys to depend on each other and beyond each other. He knew what FCA could offer the players year round. "God was telling me to be that person and coach who was there for me when I was a teenager," Chris shared. Now, Chris spends time at the school not only on the football field, but also inside the school every other week. As the FCA leader, he has an early breakfast with fifteen to twenty students before the first bell rings.

Chris's generosity started before the $500 check entered the picture, before giving money made any sense at all. In volunteering, he gave of himself to the boys on the team, doing nothing particularly notable or onerous. He just played football, something he had learned decades earlier, and acted like himself—a man holding faith in them and in the world. And the first gift—the gift of his time and skills—led to the financial gift. Which led to yet another, even bigger gift.

Like many coaches, Coach Johnson works with his student-athletes year round: football in the fall, track and field in the spring. The spring following our check giveaway, the track team was invited to participate in a national meet in Jacksonville, Florida. Many of the students had never been out of the city of Chicago; almost none had traveled outside the state of Illinois. Johnson went door-to-door asking local businesses to donate to the necessary travel expenses, but in the final week he was still $1,500 short. Johnson decided that if he could at least raise gas money, then he would drive straight through the night, saving the cost of the hotel. On a Friday afternoon he called the LaSalle church office, saying he didn't need too much, and could we help him? He planned to leave early the next morning.

There's only one answer you give to an urban high school coach producing championship teams, while financing it all with his credit card and the good will of strangers: YES! Yes. LaSalle Street Church would absolutely find the cash. We took it out of our operating funds and raced down to the South Side with the money that Friday night, trusting that the congregation would rise to cover the gift on Sunday morning.

Sunday morning, the congregation heard the whole story. We took an offering. The gifts totaled $2,300.

We've learned in our gut what our minds have learned from the researchers: Once you get a taste of how good generosity is, you just want to keep giving. And once you see the joy one person gets from giving, you want to be part of it, too.

Scientists call it social contagion theory—a way of explaining how social behaviors transfer across members of a group or network, much the way a contagious disease spreads. Although the researchers who advanced social contagion theory initially set out to understand obesity, they have since applied their findings to many other areas of life, including generosity.[4]

> Once you get a taste of how good generosity is, you just want to keep giving.

Most of us know the principle of reciprocity: you scratch my back, I'll scratch yours. We've operated under that implicit code since our youngest days on the playground—I'll push you on the swing if you push me next. Social contagion theory suggests more: that one person's behavior in a single interaction extends *beyond* the two people initially involved. Well beyond.

When it comes to generosity, one act of giving ripples out three degrees of separation.

In other words, your kind act to me today will cause me to do something generous, which in turn will inspire an act of kindness on yet another person's part, which will once again inspire an act of kindness by a fourth person. Chris Ford's first gift of volunteering eventually rippled out into the larger gift of an unimagined opportunity for the school. The gift from two members of St. Paul's church rippled out to a sick little boy hundreds of miles away.

When it comes to generosity, one act of giving ripples out three degrees of separation.

Readers of the Bible know the principle of social contagion by another name—the mustard seed. If you're a cook or a gardener, or if you've ever spread whole-grain mustard on a sandwich, you know a mustard seed measures only one or two millimeters in diameter, about the size of a pencil lead. From the pinprick of a seed, a black mustard plant matures into a bush extending up to nine feet tall. Jesus compares the kingdom of heaven to this miniscule seed: "When it is sown it grows up and becomes the greatest of all shrubs, and puts forth large branches, so that the birds of the air can make nests in its shade" (Mark 4:32). A generous act, even a seemingly insignificant one buried and unseen like the seed, births other acts reaching far beyond the original source. The smallest gesture of generosity eventually erupts in succeeding acts of love—providing shelter and rest for our fellow weary travelers on the journey of life, the same way the mustard plant offers a place for birds to nest and shade.

The power of social contagion—symbolized by the power of the mustard seed—transforms far more than football teams. The trajectory of communities, even countries, depends on individuals acting out their giving stories.

The trajectory of communities, even countries, depends on individuals acting out their giving stories.

The Mountains Ahead

Jesus tells his disciples, "If you have faith the size of a mustard seed, you will say to this mountain, 'Move from here to there,' and it will move; and nothing will be impossible for you" (Matt. 17:20).

Many of us read the passage and interpret it metaphorically. Sure, we agree we need to remain faithful, hopeful. We might even agree that God can do anything. But do we truly believe that each of us—you, me, our neighbor, anybody—can *move a mountain* with faith the size of a mustard seed?

The evidence should convince us to believe! Look at the gains made in the United Nations' Millennium Development Goals: the percent of undernourished people in developing areas has dropped by nearly half since 1990; gender disparity in education has virtually disappeared; the under-five mortality rate has dropped over 50 percent; new HIV infections have declined 40 percent; 6.2 million malaria deaths have been prevented—and that's only a sampling of the good news.[5] The mustard seeds planted in the process of drafting the millennium goals grew into deeply rooted bushes providing shade against the harsh lights of poverty and despair.

Do we truly believe that each of us—you, me, our neighbor, anybody—can move a mountain with faith the size of a mustard seed?

Yet there is more to do. Despite rising incomes, close to 30 percent of urban people in the developing world still live in slums. Six *million* children die before age five across our globe. And 42 percent of our planet's people do not have access to piped drinking water. You read that right—close to half our world's population cannot turn on a tap for fresh water.

In light of that, the good news feels a bit cheap, doesn't it? The progress seems skimpy. And the remaining challenges appear monumental. Like we took care of the easy tasks and saved the tough ones for last. Like we are facing massive mountains needing to be moved.

That's when we need to remember the mountains stood almost twice as tall just twenty years ago. And what happened? Countless people used generosity to alter the mountains' surfaces. It took work and grit and commitment and staying power. No one person single-handedly reshaped the mountains with a magical, colossal-sized backhoe. The progress was miraculous, but not magical. God whispered in the ears of a collection of laborers willing to transform the landscape, willing to let love go, over and over again. People like Bob, Sally, Manuel, Shanice, and you.

> No one person single-handedly reshaped the mountains with a magical, colossal-sized backhoe. God whispered in the ears of a collection of laborers willing to transform the landscape, willing to let love go, over and over again.

One year after our LoveLetGo check distribution, the world found itself gripped by the photograph of a three-year-old Syrian boy who had drowned and was discovered washed up along the southern shoreline of Turkey. As his story and the stories of millions of Syrian refugees filled the news wires, we at LaSalle wanted to understand what was happening and *do something* about it.

Although Syrian refugees were prevented from resettling in Chicago because of political issues, our church leaders knew we could support the plight of refugees by helping at least one family from another war-torn area to build a new life. On the first Sunday of December, church staff informed the congregation about the desire to sponsor the next new arrivals, in partnership with a local agency with a long track record in resettling people.

The goal seemed a little daunting. We needed to raise $6,000 in three weeks. The money would secure the housing and immediate expenses for a newly arriving family of three or four people. And once again, LaSalle was approaching the close of the fiscal year with a budget shortfall.

In the end, we didn't raise $6,000. We raised $39,000.

The church sent a large check to agencies providing immediate humanitarian assistance to the millions of refugees in Lebanon and Jordan. At the same time, LaSalle was informed by the local agency that a Congolese family of six—a widowed mother with her five children ranging in age from three to fifteen years old—would be arriving soon. "Their financial needs will be great," the director said. "Would it be possible for the church to assist them beyond the original $6,000 target?"

Yes! Yes, it would be possible. On the Wednesday before Easter, more than twenty LaSallers gathered at Chicago's O'Hare airport. With flags, balloons, and signs, we greeted Angelique and her five children. "We are Christians and we are Americans. Welcome to your new home!" we declared with our banners. Angelique and her family had been on the run for years. Forced by radicals to flee their home, they moved from one refugee camp to another, ending up in neighboring Rwanda.

Until they arrived at O'Hare, they had never been welcomed anywhere by anyone.

Their eyes filled with tears at the simple sight of seeing

people happy to meet them. With wide smiles, the children put on the coats and gloves we had brought with us. But they weren't the only ones crying and smiling. Other passengers and families in the terminal kept approaching us, asking, "Who are you? Where are you from? Why are you doing this?" Our explanations seemed to be met with a sense of yearning. They wanted to be part of a story like this, too. They wanted to love and let go.

The story of generosity unfolds around us daily. On football fields, at airport terminals, and in elementary school classrooms. While generosity's story unfolded in the most unlikely of circumstances at LaSalle Street Church, its ending is one God certainly predicted for our church and predicts for all of us: generosity frees us to be our truest selves—*generous people who flourish in the act of giving.* As the apostle Paul wrote, "Love never ends. . . . And now faith, hope, and love abide, these three; and the greatest of these is love" (1 Cor. 13:8, 13).

Generosity frees us to be our truest selves—generous people who flourish in the act of giving.

The greatest of these is love. Our church, a generous church overflowing with generous people, understood Paul's message. We loved and let go. You can too.

AＦTＥRWOＲD

After nine months of discernment, the members of LaSalle Street Church voted to approve the following distribution of the remaining $1.44 million after its LoveLetGo tithe of $160,000 to the congregants:

Supporting the Local Community
- $160,000 to neighborhood churches and organizations addressing social and racial justice in Chicago
- $125,000 to a financial wellness partnership administered by Cabrini-Green Legal Aid (see Chapter 8)
- $125,000 to LaSalle Neighbors ministry to expand outreach to the immediate community
- $25,000 to Art on Sedgwick (founded by a LaSalle member), an art center designed to foster connection across racial and socioeconomic lines

Supporting Global Neighbors
- $100,000 to the Institute for Global Impact (founded by a long-time LaSalle missionary) for training of pastoral and public leaders in East Africa

- $100,000 to the World Vision effort in Tanzania to transform smallholder farms through irrigation
- $30,000 to the Bussy-St.-George church building fund in support of LaSalle missionaries whose near-Paris church, made up largely of African immigrants, has outgrown its space

Sustaining LaSalle

- $400,000 to the Cornerstone Center renovation to enable more and better service to the 1000+ people entering the building daily
- $175,000 in seed money for a future capital campaign to sustain the nineteenth-century sanctuary building
- $100,000 to create a sustainability fund to address financing and/or capital needs for the community center building, as determined by the Property & Finance committee

Investing in People

- $70,000 to the Low Cost Fund, available to congregants who have an idea for a program or ministry and need a small amount of funding to launch
- $20,000 to the Travel Fund to financially assist congregants who seek to take an international mission or vision trip
- $10,000 for LaSalle Street Church staff development

Qᵤᴇꜱᴛɪᴏɴꜱ ꜰᴏʀ Rᴇꜰʟᴇᴄᴛɪᴏɴ ᴀɴᴅ Dɪꜱᴄᴜꜱꜱɪᴏɴ

Chapter 1

The benefits of a generous life are demonstrative, verifiable, and authentic. And they're all right within our grasp—no matter how little or how much we have. At the end of the day, we seem to be hard-wired to give.

In the most recent available data on tithing rates — defined as giving 10 percent or more of annual income to religious or non-profit organizations — the Barna Group showed 5 percent of American adults in 2012 had tithed.

1. The authors cite research verifying the linkage between generosity and several measures of well-being. What research conclusions do you find most interesting and why?
2. If generosity is a super-power, how are you exercising that power? In what ways do you give now, and how do you hope to give in the future?
3. As the Barna statistic above shows, few adults in the U.S.

tithe. What is your personal, religious, or corporate experience with tithing, if any? What do you believe prevents more of us from tithing, when the benefits of generosity are so compelling?

Chapter 2

Not hard or heroic, generosity at LaSalle simply began with awareness. This is how generosity always begins. Every day, even when squeezed by scarcity, we receive opportunities to view the world from the vantage point of generosity. Generosity reorients us to others and to our own contexts. Generosity allows us to step boldly and humbly into a greater narrative where our actions move the plot forward. Generosity grants us the freedom and perspective to be the beggar telling another beggar where to find food.

In 2012, 388 million people in Sub-Saharan Africa lived in extreme poverty, earning U.S. $1.90 or less per day. That number represented 42 percent of the area's population (World Bank's Poverty Overview).

1. *Scarcity,* the authors suggest, is a relative term, and our perspective on its definition shifts when we practice generosity. When have you felt the pressure of scarcity? What, if anything, caused your perspective to change?

2. Despite other financial needs, LaSalle Street Church still made its $1,000 investment in Atrium Village. How do you approach similar trade-offs in your own life, when practical concerns appear to conflict with a compelling cause or investment?

3. We read about Laura Thomas and her neighbor in Tanzania. What elements of her story most struck you? Why? How does the statistic above about poverty in Sub-Saharan Africa affect your response to her story now?

Chapter 3

Our very first framing story is the story of a generous God who freely yields everything to us. There was enough for the earth to flourish and for people to prosper. We were invited to take part in a very good world. Leaning into this framing story has all sorts of implications for how human life is constructed. It means that before we were gripped by the fear of scarcity, we knew the reality of abundance; before we felt the spasm of self-protection, we felt the pleasure of plenty. And before there was a story of human isolation and fear, there was a bigger and greater story of community and blessing.

In 2015, the bottom 50 percent of adults in the world held less than 1 percent of the world's wealth, according to Credit

Suisse's Global Wealth Report 2015. What did it take to be in the top half? Only U.S. $3,210 in net worth.

1. Abundance and scarcity often fight for the right to be our framing story. Where have you seen evidence of this conflict in your life? What events or circumstances trigger fear in you or in the people around you?

2. Despite losing all of the church's parking options, LaSalle Street Church's board chose not to spend the windfall on a parking solution. When have you had to exercise similar faith and trust that your immediate needs would be met?

3. The authors suggest our generation has the power to erase global poverty if we live into our framing story of abundance. How does the statistic above—that $3,210 in net worth puts a person in the top half of the world's wealthiest people—reframe your perspective on abundance? What is the relevance today of the apostle Paul's words: "Your surplus is for their need, and their need is for your surplus"?

Chapter 4

Remembering who we are poses a challenge not just to people (and animals) in the fictional world; the theme speaks to us because we find ourselves asking similiar questions of identity: Who am I? What's important to me? How am I supposed to live my life?

In 2014, Americans age fifteen and older spent, on average, seventeen minutes relaxing and thinking every day, as determined by the Bureau of Labor Statistics' annual Time Use Survey.

1. Make an inventory of the various identities you wear each day. Do you find practicing generosity easier or harder with each identity?
2. David Melia discovered his core identity at a young age. Do you feel you understand your core identity? If not, how might you re-discover it?
3. LaSalle Street Church spent nine months in discernment, much of the time focused on identifying its core DNA. If connecting to our core identities is critical to practicing generosity, how much time should we devote to reflection? Would seventeen minutes relaxing and thinking a day suffice?

Chapter 5

The longing for connection and relationship contrasts with our typical transactions—much of the time we actively avoid establishing connection. . . . Given the ease with which we can avoid interactions, we might wonder if any attempt to live relationally is fighting a losing battle. But in the generous life, proximity and relationship matter.

Empathy offered in the virtual world—on social media, or via text or email—is one-sixth as effective in helping the recipient feel supported than empathy provided in the real world with a hug or a kind word, according to a study from California State University.

1. The authors propose that the ability to understand others' needs requires getting close to them. Who might you have the opportunity to get close to?
2. The presence of money on our minds, even subconsciously, primes us to act independently. In what ways can you counteract this natural impulse?
3. Consider the role of technology in your life. How has technology enabled you to connect to others, like Eric Larson did with Fatou? How has technology hampered your connection with others?

Chapter 6

Arresting the feelings of scarcity comes only by giving. When we feel cash poor, we sense we're richer by giving money away. When we feel short on time, we perceive ourselves freer when we volunteer our hours. When we feel sapped of emotional energy, we become refueled by attending closely to another person's life. The psychological research supports this truth, but likely you've experienced this in your life already. Generosity resets the saturation point and offers contentment—in plenty and in need.

Personal bankruptcy filings totaled nearly 820,000 in 2015, compared to 287,000 in 1980, as reported by the American Bankruptcy Institute.

1. Have you established a financial saturation point for yourself? If so, how did you arrive at your decision? If not, what factors might influence your perception of your saturation point?

2. How do you explain the statistic above on the number of personal bankruptcy cases in the U.S.? What societal pressures work against the saturation point? Against generosity?

3. We heard about Kristen Metz and Stephen Martin, both people who could have used their $500 LoveLetGo checks to address their own financial needs. What do you believe motivated them to give away the funds?

4. Have you experienced a time when you gave something away despite feeling constrained? How do you feel now about the situation as you reflect back on it?

Chapter 7

It's one thing to live untouched by the world in the first century. It's quite another thing when we've been drinking from a fire hose of information in the twenty-first century. Yet the antidote remains the same: Stop. Wait. Be still. Listen.

Mindfulness. Contemplation. Meditation. Silence. Prayer. These were the habits we LaSallers needed if we were going to get to the other side of generosity.

According to the Institute of Medicine, 50 to 70 million U.S. adults have a sleep or wakefulness disorder. Sleep insufficiency may be due to round-the-clock access to technology and work schedules, as well as insomnia and sleep apnea.

1. How frequently are you able to stop, wait, and listen? What barriers do you face in finding time for silence, mindfulness, and prayer? How could you grant yourself increased permission for times of quiet and solitude?
2. How do you believe our culture helps or hinders our ability to be still?
3. Most of us understand the negative impact of sleep deprivation on our attention span and our physical health. How might sleep deprivation impact our spiritual health? What evidence of this impact have you seen in your life?

Chapter 8

Listening wisely opens us to generosity — generosity expressed and generosity received. When we listen expectantly, we begin to conceive Big Ideas from small stories, like salary increases for forty people or five loaves feeding five thousand. Careful listening allows us to remember that there is a broader narrative in progress, and in our listening, we may even catch a glimpse of the role we have been asked to play.

Psychology Today reports that disturbing news stories outnumber positive news stories in the media by a ratio of as high as fourteen to one.

1. The authors outline three processes in this chapter: listening wisely to the world's needs, filtering out the ideas meant for us to hear, and taking our first steps. Which of these activities do you find most challenging and why?

2. We learned about Paul Hettinga and Larry Reed's idea, and about the deviation from the original plan that occurred as they pursued their idea. Have you ever felt thwarted in your efforts at generosity? How did you handle the situation? What did you discover in the process?

3. What stories or concerns has your spirit been most sensitive toward lately? How might you engage more deeply with those nudges?

Chapter 9

Throughout this book we've tied generosity to a way of living that is freeing. We've used the word deliberately because that's how people describe what generosity has meant to them. There is a sense of contentment, a thread of connectedness, a joy and a peace that have rooted themselves into the soil of their lives. All together it adds up to freedom.

People who practice gratitude spend less time making social comparisons—noting what other people have relative to them. This finding has been replicated across several psychological studies.

1. When do you most often find yourself expressing gratitude? In what situations do you find it difficult to express gratitude?
2. The authors share stories of gratitude connecting people across time. In what way has someone else's act of gratitude imprinted you?
3. This chapter is about gratitude, yet the quotation above speaks to the concept of freedom. What links gratitude to freedom? How have you seen that linkage manifest in your life?

Chapter 10

Generosity doesn't require a formal community. All that's required is an openness to listening and a willingness to engage. That's it. You don't need to have the heart of a saint; you already have a giver's heart. You don't need a hefty bank balance; you already live in a world of abundance. You don't need to develop a particular talent or skill; you've already been given a role to play in the grand narrative of generosity.

The vast majority of charitable contributions—81 percent—are made by individuals rather than foundations or corporations, according to Giving USA's 2014 report.

1. What causes you to be optimistic about the ability of one individual to make a difference in the world? How can you increase your exposure to these sources of optimism?
2. The disciples had five fish and two loaves of bread. What resources of time, skills, money, and relationships do you have?
3. When have you loved and let go? Where would you next like to love and let go?

FOR FURTHER READING

For evidence that generosity is good for us:

The Paradox of Generosity: Giving We Receive, Grasping We Lose by Christian Smith and Hilary Anne Davidson (Oxford: Oxford University Press, 2014).

To understand the powers and weaknesses of our lightning-fast brains:

Thinking, Fast and Slow by Daniel Kahneman (New York: Farrar, Straus & Giroux, 2011).

To engage in deeper listening:

The Way of Discernment: Spiritual Practices for Decision Making by Elizabeth Liebert (Louisville: Westminster John Knox Press, 2008).

For insight into generosity's impact on your career:

Give and Take: Why Helping Others Drives Our Success by Adam Grant (New York: Penguin Books, 2014).

For a synthesis of research on meaning and interactions:
Are You Fully Charged? The Three Keys to Energizing Your Work and Life by Tom Rath (Arlington, VA: Silicon Guild, 2015).

The Good $ense ministry (www.goodsensemovement.org) offers practical resources on money management for individuals, groups, and churches.

The Barna Group (www.barna.org) issues regular research on American donor trends.

Notes

Notes to Chapter 1

1. Christian Smith and Hilary Anne Davidson, *The Paradox of Generosity* (Oxford: Oxford University Press, 2014), p. 4.

2. Smith and Davidson, *Paradox of Generosity*, p. 47.

3. Michael Norton and Elizabeth Dunn, *Happy Money: The Science of Happier Spending* (New York: Simon & Schuster), p. 120.

4. Norton and Dunn, *Happy Money*, p. 113.

5. George Vaillant, *Triumphs of Experience* (Cambridge, MA: Belknap Press, 2015), p. 27.

6. All the personal narratives featured in this book are used with full permission. Some names in the narratives may have been changed.

Notes to Chapter 2

1. Charles Hogren and Steve Ujvarosy contributed significantly to our knowledge and understanding of LaSalle Street Church history.

2. Daniel Kahneman, *Thinking, Fast and Slow* (New York: Farrar, Straus and Giroux, 2011).

3. Randy Wang, http://www.cs.princeton.edu/~rywang/berkeley/258/parable.html. Accessed 19 October 2016.

4. Mary MacVean, "For Many People, Gathering Possessions Is Just the Stuff of Life," *Los Angeles Times*, March 21, 2014. http://articles.latimes.com/2014/mar/21/health/la-he-keeping-stuff-20140322. Accessed 30 January 2016.

5. UN AIDS Fact Sheet 2015.

6. United Republic of Tanzania, Global AIDS Response Country Progress Report, March 31, 2014. http://files.unaids.org/en/dataanalysis/knowyourresponse/countryprogressreports/2014countries/TZA_narrative_report_2014.pdf. Accessed 19 October 2016.

7. National Bureau of Statistics (NBS) [Tanzania] and Macro International Inc., *Tanzania HIV/AIDS and Malaria Indicator Survey: Key Findings* (Calverton, MD: NBS and Macro International Inc., 2009).

Notes to Chapter 3

1. https://www.usaid.gov/ending-extreme-poverty. Accessed 19 October 2016.
2. Shane Claiborne, Facebook post, Nov. 7, 2014.

Notes to Chapter 4

1. LaSalle Street Church member Lenora Rand named the campaign, and we thank her for blessing its use in this book's title.
2. Elizabeth Liebert, *The Way of Discernment: Spiritual Practices for Decision Making* (Louisville: Westminster John Knox Press, 2008), p. 23.

Notes to Chapter 5

1. Information on and quotation from Christopher Jacobs sourced from Rick Kogan, "Sharp Focus: Class for Cook County Jail Inmates Develops into Local Photographer's Passion," *Chicago Tribune*, Feb. 14, 2016, Section 4, p. 1.
2. Kogan, "Sharp Focus," *Chicago Tribune*.
3. Kathleen D. Vohs, Nicole L. Mead, and Miranda R. Goode, "The Psychological Consequences of Money," *Science*, 17 November 2006: no page number. http://science.sciencemag.org/content/314/5802/1154. Accessed 19 October 2016.
4. Interestingly, people who are primed with financial distress (low money rather than high money) behave more like unprimed subjects. This finding reminds us of "the beggar that helps another beggar find bread."
5. Tom Rath, *Are You Fully Charged? The Three Keys to Energizing Your Work and Life* (Arlington, VA: Silicon Guild, 2015).

Notes to Chapter 6

1. http://www.nerdwallet.com/blog/credit-card-data/average-credit
-card-debt-household/. Accessed 19 October 2016.

2. http://www.startribune.com/feeling-secure-is-about-more-than
-money/308519041/. Accessed 19 October 2016.

3. http://www.cnbc.com/2015/05/06/naires-say-theyre-middle-class
.html. Accessed 19 October 2016.

4. Psychologists call this phenomenon "hedonic adaptation."

5. http://www.forbes.com/sites/learnvest/2012/04/24/the-salary-that
-will-make-you-happy-hint-its-less-than-75000/#d47c2e547cf7. Accessed
19 October 2016.

Notes to Chapter 7

1. http://earthsky.org/human-world/martin-hilbert-all-human
-information-stored-on-cd-would-reach-beyond-the-moon. Accessed
19 October 2016.

2. Eyal Ophir, Clifford Nass, and Anthony D. Wagner, "Cognitive Control in Media Multitasking," *Proceedings of the National Academy of Sciences
of the United States*, 19 Sept. 2008, no page number. http://www.pnas.org/
content/106/37/15583.full. Accessed 19 October 2016.

3. http://pss.sagepub.com/content/23/10/1130.short. Accessed 19 October 2016.

Notes to Chapter 8

1. http://www.today.com/series/2015-voices/gravity-payments-ceo
-dan-price-reflects-70k-minimum-salary-experiment-t64401. Accessed 19
October 2016.

2. https://www.glassdoor.com/research/ceo-pay-ratio/. Accessed 19
October 2016.

3. Marilyn Hargis, "On the Road: The Inns and Outs of Travel in
First-Century Palestine," *Christianity Today* Library, July 1, 1998. http://
www.ctlibrary.com/ch/issues/issue-59/on-road.html. Accessed 19 October
2016.

4. http://www.calledthejourney.com/blog/2014/12/17/frederick
-buechner-on-calling. Accessed 19 October 2016.

Notes to Chapter 9

1. Robert Emmons and Michael McCullough, "Counting Blessings versus Burdens: An Experimental Investigation of Gratitude and Subjective Well-Being in Daily Life," *Journal of Personality and Social Psychology* 84, no. 2 (2003): no page number. http://greatergood.berkeley.edu/pdfs/ GratitudePDFs/6Emmons-BlessingsBurdens.pdf. Accessed 19 October 2016.

2. C. V. O. Witvliet, T. E. Ludwig, and D. J. Bauer, "Please Forgive Me: Transgressors' Emotions and Physiology during Imagery of Seeking Forgiveness and Victim Responses," *Journal of Psychology and Christianity* 21 (2002): 219-33. http://digitalcommons.hope.edu/cgi/viewcontent .cgi?article=2302&context=faculty_publications. Accessed 19 October 2016.

3. Malcolm Gladwell, *Outliers: The Story of Success* (New York: Back Bay Books, 2008), p. 42.

4. *Cross Currents* 50, no. 3 (Fall 2000). http://www.crosscurrents.org/ madsenfoo.htm. Accessed 19 October 2016.

Notes to Chapter 10

1. http://www.chicagotribune.com/news/local/ct-lasalle-street
-church-reverse-tithing-met-20141224-story.html. Accessed 19 October 2016.

2. http://www.naacp.org/pages/criminal-justice-fact-sheet. Accessed 19 October 2016.

3. For more on Chris Ford's story, see the video: https://www.youtube .com/watch?v=hKeoHeeYKcI. Accessed 19 October 2016.

4. James H. Fowler and Nicholas A. Christakis, "Cooperative Behavior Cascades in Human Social Networks," *Proceedings of the National Academy of Sciences of the United States of America* 107, no. 12 (2010): 334-338. PMC. Web. 22 Apr. 2016. http://www.ncbi.nlm.nih.gov/pmc/articles/ PMC2851803/. Accessed 19 October 2016.

5. http://www.un.org/millenniumgoals/2015_MDG_Report/pdf/ MDG%202015%20rev%20(July%201).pdf. Accessed 19 October 2016.

Acknowledgments

This book contains stories about what happens when regular people decide to practice countercultural, radical generosity. We are fortunate to be part of a church filled with just such people. We thank everyone at LaSalle for allowing their lives to illustrate and to inspire. Your reach has extended far, far beyond your grasp.

We bear the mark of an earlier generation of generous radicals at LaSalle. People who prayed and dreamed, who gave generously to a future they never saw. The leaders of our Loaves & Fishes project carried on their predecessors' tradition of generosity. We thank all of them, especially the eminently capable, doggedly faithful Amber Johnson. We are indebted as well to LaSallers Becky Haase and Oreon Trickey for their invaluable support as early readers of our manuscript.

Our North Star on this book journey has been editor Lil Copan. She believed in the power of the LoveLetGo story, and believed in our ability to express it. We handed her a composition in the rough—with measures out of order and notes careening off the staff—and she made it sing. We value her as mentor, coach, guide, and beloved dinner companion, and we hope this book honors her as much as it honors the LaSalle community.

Her marvelous colleague, Mary Hietbrink, also merits high praise as a maestro of finesse, adding the prose equivalents of crescendos and codas and ensuring the composition would play beautifully in the mind of the reader. Bravo!

Our deepest thank you undoubtedly goes to our husbands, Terry Truax and Chris Campbell. They love us despite our ungenerous moments (which occurred with regularity during our intense writing periods). Both men have given themselves over to God, to us, and to our cherished families. We are privileged to share our lives with them.

Motherhood teaches generosity in a way nothing else can. We thank our children—Sumner, Porter, Burnley, Helen, and Lydia—for the powerful lessons we have learned in growing them up.

Our lives are full of entirely regular, entirely amazing people. They are the best people we know. How grateful we are.